MICHAEL AND HIS LOST ANGEL

A PLAY IN FIVE ACTS

BY

HENRY ARTHUR JONES

AUTHOR OF "THE TEMPTER," "THE CRUSADERS," "THE CASE OF REBELLIOUS SUSAN," "THE MIDDLEMAN," "THE DANCING GIRL," "JUDAH," "THE MASQUERADERS," "THE TRIUMPH OF THE PHILISTINES," ETC.

New York
THE MACMILLAN COMPANY
LONDON: MACMILLAN & CO., Ltd.
1909

All rights reserved

COPYRIGHT, 1895,
BY MACMILLAN AND CO.

Set up and electrotyped. Published May, 1896. Reprinted November, 1905; March, 1909.

Norwood Press
J. S. Cushing & Co. — Berwick & Smith Co.
Norwood, Mass., U.S.A.

This scarce antiquarian book is included in our special *Legacy Reprint Series*. In the interest of creating a more extensive selection of rare historical book reprints, we have chosen to reproduce this title even though it may possibly have occasional imperfections such as missing and blurred pages, missing text, poor pictures, markings, dark backgrounds and other reproduction issues beyond our control. Because this work is culturally important, we have made it available as a part of our commitment to protecting, preserving and promoting the world's literature.

PREFACE

MICHAEL, though styled by Milton "of celestial armies prince," has found his sword unequal to the task of combating the well-ordered hosts of darkness,

> By thousands and by millions ranged for fight.

The author of "Michael and his Lost Angel" seeks accordingly in print consolation for the rebuffs he has experienced upon the stage. Some comfort in the midst of defeat may be found in the fact that the gods themselves fight vainly against prejudice and stupidity. I am not in the least seeking to set aside the verdict pronounced by the majority of "experts" upon Mr. Jones's latest play and subsequently accepted if not ratified by the general public which would not be induced to see it. All I seek to do is to deal so far as I am able with the adverse influences to which it succumbed, and to explain why I think it a fine work and in many respects a triumph.

PREFACE

The misfortunes of "Michael and his Lost Angel" attended, if they did not anticipate, its conception. Like Marina in Pericles it had at least

as chiding a nativity

as play has often encountered. Before it saw the light a war had been waged concerning its name. That the name itself involved as some seemed to think a gratuitous insult to any form of religious connection or was even ill chosen I am not prepared to grant. Michael is not a scriptural character, and his functions, civil and militant, and his place in the celestial hierarchy are assigned him by uninspired writers. But for the use made of him in art and by Milton it is doubtful whether his name would be familiar enough to the general public to provoke a discussion. A discussion was, however, provoked and with a portion of those present the verdict was pronounced before the piece had been given. An opening scene, meanwhile, in which the very raison-d'être of the play is found, an indispensable portion of the motive began too soon and was, through the noise and disturbance caused by late arrivals, practically unheard. The difficulty thus caused was never quite overcome, and the nature of Michael Feversham's offence and the value of his expiation were both partially misunderstood.

That the display of human passions in a sacred edifice and the lavish use of ecclesiastical ceremonial might cause offence I could have conceived, had there not been the immediately previous proof of the success of another play in which the very words of the Inspired Teacher are used with a background of pagan revelry and a lavish and superfluous display of nudity of limb. Paul of Tarsus is surely a more recognisable personage, and one more closely connected with Christian faith than a nebulous being such as Michael. While, however, the slight banter in the title of Mr. Jones's play and the reproduction of the rather florid pageant of the highest Anglican service has in a work of earnest purpose and masterly execution wounded sensitive consciences, the presentation as vulgar as inept of a portion of the holiest mysteries of religion has been received with sacerdotal benediction as well as with public applause. Foreign opinion concerning English hypocrisy and prudery finds frequent utterance, and our witty Gallic neighbours have excogitated a word they believe to be English and take as the cant phrase of the Briton, *schoking*. We do at times our best to furnish foreigners with a justification for their views; and in the present case at least, we have shown our capacity to "strain at a gnat and swallow a camel."

That the author has overburdened his work with dialogue is shown by the result, since a play that the public will not have is naturally a play unsuited to the public.

Some measure of the blame, to my thinking, almost the whole of the blame, rests with the audience. In seeking to interest his world in a series of duologues Mr. Jones has credited it with a knowledge of dramatic art and an interest in psychology it does not possess. His experiment is analogous to that undertaken in France by the younger Dumas. A *première* of Dumas was one of the most fashionable and intellectual of Parisian "functions." With ears sharpened to acutest attention the Parisian public listened not only to dialogue thrice as long as any Mr. Jones has attempted, but also to monologue of the most didactic kind. In the case of Victor Hugo again there is more than one soliloquy of length absolutely portentous. These things have never wearied a public art-loving, theatre-loving, before all appreciative of literary subtlety and conscious of what are the true springs of dramatic interest.

At the moment when these lines are written, the London playgoer, not perhaps of the most fashionable class, receives with delight a scene in which a hero swims to the rescue of injured innocence, which a generation ago established the fortunes of a dramatist and a theatre. I refer, of course, to the Colleen Bawn of Dion Boucicault, which has once more been revived. The rescue scene in this hit exactly the sense of the English public and fulfilled its ideal. For a year or two afterwards the intellect of our dramatists was exercised as to the means by which virtue imperilled could be rescued, whether by climbing a tower or swinging by a tree, or by any other contrivance involving the risk of a broken neck. Those days, happily, are past. We have not, however, made great progress in our education, and seem yet to have to learn that the most telling drama is the psychological, and that dialogue moves us, or should move us, more than incident. Othello, in some respects the most poignant of tragedies, is nearly all duologue, the gradual poisoning of the Moor's mind by Iago being one of the most tremendous scenes ever attempted. The Greeks, the great art-loving people of antiquity, banished in tragedy all incident from the stage, and in this respect have been copied by the great school of French classicists.

So far, without any very direct purpose or intention, I have been posing, apparently, as the apologist for Mr. Jones's play. Underneath this, perhaps, some few may have traced a design still less definite of apologising for the English public. Nothing is further from my intention than to proffer an excuse for what I regard as a fine and most moving drama. For myself, I can only say that rarely indeed have my entrails been stirred by more forcible pathos, my attention been rapt by more inspiriting a theme, and my intellect been satisfied by dialogue more natural, appropriate, and, in the highest sense, dramatic. In one respect, I am disposed at times to agree with some of Mr. Jones's censors. The logic of events which brings about the scene in the island is, perhaps, not sufficiently inexorable. That Mrs. Lesden is, in the eyes of the world, hopelessly compromised when she spends a night alone on the island with her lover, I will concede. I can conceive, however, Michael treating her with the more delicacy therefor, abandoning to her his house, and spending a summer night, no enormous penalty, in the open air, on the seashore.

This, however, only means that the overmastering influence of passion over Michael has not been fully exhibited in action.

With Mr. Jones's previous works — with "Judah," "The Crusaders," "Saints and Sinners" — "Michael and his Lost Angel" is connected by strong, albeit not too evident, links. The bent of Mr. Jones's mind, or the effect of his early environment, seems to force him into showing the struggle between religious or priestly training, and high and sincere aspiration, on the one hand, and, on the other, those influences, half earthly, half divine, of our physical nature, which sap where they cannot escalade, and, in the highest natures, end always in victory. There is nothing in Michael Feversham of the hypocrite, little even of the Puritan. Subject from the outset to priestly influences, and wedded to theories of asceticism, the more binding as self-imposed, he has come to look upon the renegation of the most imperative as well as, in one sense, the holiest functions of our nature as the condition of moral regeneration. *Sic itur ad astra.* Crime, generally, he holds as condemnable, but murder and theft are things aloof from the human nature with which he has to deal. They are exceptional products of diseased organisations or untoward surroundings. Not one of his flock that he is conducting peacefully and unwittingly to Rome, is coming to him to own in confession to having stolen an umbrella from a rack or a book from a stall, still less to having slain his enemy on a secret path. Had such confession been made, it would have been an episode of comparatively little interest, a mere skirmish in the war he constantly sustains against the forces of evil. Uncleanness, on the other hand, as he elects to describe it, is the one offence against the higher life, in regard to which, whether as concerns inward promptings or outside manifestation, it behooves him to be ever armed and vigilant. Accepting this theory, which, though subversive of the highest and most obvious aims of nature, is still held by a considerable section of civilised humanity, the conduct of Michael wins a measure of sympathy. In imposing upon Rose Gibbard the unutterably shameful and humiliating penance, the nature of which reaches us from the ferocious Calvinism of the Puritan rather than from the gentler moral discipline of the Romish church, to which he is hastening, Michael is thoroughly sincere and conscientious. He believes it the best, nay, the only way to save her soul and restore her to the self-respect and dignity of pure womanhood. So much in earnest is he that, when Mrs. Lesden propounds the theory, which among the virtuous and generous wins acceptance, that "it is nearly always the good girls who are betrayed," he resents the utterance as a levity, not to say a profanity. A character such as this is not only conceivable, it is well known. There is nothing in its psychology to scare the unthinking or alarm the vulgar. In the humiliation which Michael is himself compelled to undergo, I find at once the vindication of a morality immeasurably higher and more Christian than that taught by any of the churches, and a soul tragedy of the most harrowing description. My words will to some appear irreverent. I am sorry, but I cannot help it. It is not I who said of the woman taken in adultery, "Qui sine peccato est vestrum, primus in illa lapidem mittat"; and again, "Nec ego te condemnabo. Vade et jam amplius noli peccare."

That a nature such as that of Michael would be likely to provoke the curiosity and interest of an Audrie Lesden, few will contest. Vain, frivolous, passionate, mutinous, sceptical, defeated, unhappy, with the sweet milk of true womanhood curdled in her breast, Audrie Lesden sets herself the task of breaking through the defences of this " marble saint." She succeeds. Under her temptations the icy image thaws. That she herself thaws also, is a matter of which she scarcely takes cognisance. In her mood of irritation and defiance what happens to herself is a matter of comparative indifference. She has abandoned her positions and called in her reserves, concentrating all her forces for a combat, in which victory is, if possible, more disastrous than rout.

Let us take then the position. A man resolute as he thinks in the maintenance of a standard of scarcely possible and wholly undesirable purity, a woman bent at first in wantonness of spirit upon his subjugation, but finding as she progresses that her heart is in the struggle, and that instead of being engaged in a mere sportive encounter she is playing for her life, her all. Here are the materials for a tragedy, and a tragedy is the outcome. The idea is happy, the execution is superb, and the result is a play that must be pronounced so far Mr. Jones's masterpiece, and that is in effect one of the worthiest and in the highest sense of the word, putting apart the financial result and judging only from the standpoint of art, one of the most successful dramas of the age. For the first time the dramatist has divested himself of all adventitious aid or support, swimming boldly and skilfully on the sea of drama. The melodramatic devices on which he has leant disappear, the sketches of eccentric character by which he strove to fortify past stories have vanished. A tale of ill-starred love is told with simple downright earnestness, simplicity, and good faith. Not a character unnecessary to the action is introduced, not a word that is superfluous or rhetorical is spoken. Free from obstruction, unpolluted and undefiled, a limpid stream of human life and love flows into the ocean of defeat and death.

In some respects the loves of Michael Feversham and Audrie Lesden seem to take rank with the masterpieces of human passion, if not with Romeo and Juliet, with Cupid and Psyche, with Paul and Virginia, and shall I add with Edgar of Ravenswood and Lucy Ashton, at least with Helen and Paris, Antony and Cleopatra, and Manon Lescaut and the Chevalier des Grieux. Just enough of fatefulness as well as of human wilfulness is there to add the crowning grace of tragedy by showing man the sport of circumstance. Michael dwells on this point and finds "a curious bitter amusement" in tracing out the sequence of events. "The hundred little chances, accidents as we call them, that gave us to each other. Everything I did to avoid you threw me at your feet. I felt myself beginning to love you. I wrote urgently to Uncle Ned in Italy, thinking I'd tell him and that he would save me. He came. I couldn't tell him of you, but his coming kept Withycombe [the boatman] from getting your telegram. I went to Saint Decuman's to escape from you. You were moved to come to me. I sent away my own boat to put the sea between us: and so I imprisoned you with me. Six years ago I used all my influence to have the new lighthouse built on Saint Margaret's Isle instead of Saint Decuman's, so that I might keep Saint Decuman's lonely for myself and prayer. I kept it lonely for myself and you. It was what we call a chance I didn't go to Saint Margaret's with Andrew and my uncle. It was what we call a chance that you telegraphed to my boatman instead of your own. If any one thing had gone differently —" Even so. In this world, however, "nothing walks with aimless feet" and the most commonplace and least significant of our actions may have world-reaching results.

"Oh, God bring back yesterday" is the despairing cry which, since the beginning of time, has been wrung from human lips.

The scene on the island seems to me admirable in management. I am not sure that I care for Audrie's confession concerning the conquest of the heart of "a cherub aged ten," though that leads to the very humorous illustration of his sister's treason. Michael's own confession on the other hand of his one flirtation with Nelly, the tender osculation never repeated, and her farewell words "Goodnight, Mike" serve a distinct purpose in preparing Michael's ultimate subjugation. "She called you Mike?" says Audrie with some surprise and more bitterness. He is human then, this austere, ice-bound man only just beginning to relent to her. His lips, those lips for which she hungers, have been pressed upon a woman's face, and he has had a boy's name by which another woman has dared to call him, a name her own lips tremble to frame. She is long before she does frame it aloud. The idea of that woman however dwells in her mind, and its full influence and the extent of her surrender are shown when at what might be quite, and is almost, the close of the third act she looks back and says, "Listen to this. Whatever happens, I shall never belong to anybody but you. You understand? I shall never belong to anybody but you, MIKE." All this is supreme in tenderness and truthfulness and is the more dramatic and convincing on account of its simplicity.

So it is throughout the play. There is not a moment when the effort after rhetorical speech interferes with or mars the downright earnestness and conviction of the language and the fervour of the underlying emotion. The love-making so far as we are permitted to see it is on the woman's side. Hers are the raptures, the reproaches, the protestations. Only in the moment of supreme difficulty or defeat is Michael tortured into amorous utterance, and then even it is the idea of responsibility and possession that weighs upon him. The deed is done, he belongs to the woman with whom he has sinned, the past is ineffaceable: no expiation can alter, even if it may atone. He is, moreover, impenitent in the midst of penitence, fiercely glad, fiercely happy, in what he has done, ready to face all tribulation, loss, and reproach, rather than sacrifice the burning, maddening, joyous knowledge of his guilt. This is the spirit in which love in strong, austere, unemotional natures manifests itself. "All for love or the world well lost" is the title Dryden gives his alteration of Antony and Cleopatra. All for love or heaven well lost is the phrase Mr. Jones in effect puts into the lips of his Michael, a phrase used not for the first time, and savouring of blasphemy or sanctity according to the point of view of the audience.

There are perhaps higher ideals of love. What dramatist or preacher has said anything finer than the words of the great cavalier lyrist: —

> I could not love thee, dear, so much,
> Loved I not honour more.

One of the best known of the Tudor dramatists, Habington, says: —

> He is but
> A coward lover, whom or death or hell
> Can fright from 's Mistress.

The enormity of Michael's sacrifice, the very unpardonableness of his offence, constitute the sweetest savour to him as to her. To her it brings an intoxicating, a delirious triumph, to him a sense how much he must hug to himself and cherish a possession secured at so fearful a price.

PREFACE

It is perhaps the distinguishing characteristic of Michael's madness that the sin once committed is not repented. Landor talks of

> Modesty who when she flies
> Is fled for ever.

This is true of other things beside modesty. Not seldom it is true of virtue. Sin is our sad portion, let us make the best of it. If we may not have a "stately pleasure-house" of love, let us get what shelter we may and at least cling close together while the winds of censure rebuke and the rains of scandal chill. This is, of course, what Audrie would suggest. "My beloved is mine and I am his." What matter concerning other things, what other thing is there to matter? Not so Michael. Lead me back, he says, to the ways of peace and purity. Let us march hand in hand to the throne of forgiveness. There is no such throne, says the moralist and the priest within him. "Can one be pardoned and retain the offence?" he asks with Claudius, and the answer extracted from his conscience is a negative. After her death, a death for which he is, as he knows, mainly responsible, he abandons all struggle, resigns his volition and his being into the hands of a church that demands implicit obedience and pardons no questioning of its decisions and decrees, and taking upon himself monastic vows enters permanently a cloister.

If this is not according to the present reading of the word "tragedy," I know not where tragedy is to be sought. It may be that the subject is one that cannot with advantage be set before the public with the fierce and brilliant illumination of stage presentation. Compare however the method of treatment, earnest, severe, resolute, unfaltering, with that which was adopted by novelists dealing with clerical trials and offences of the sort from the time of Diderot to that of L'Abbé Michon, the reputed author of "La Réligieuse," "Le Maudit," and other works of the class.

Once more I repeat that "Michael and his Lost Angel" is the best play Mr. Jones has given the stage and is in the full sense a masterpiece. It is the work of a man conscious of strength, and sure of the weapons he employs. Whether the stage will know it again who shall say? It will at least take rank as literature and in its present shape appeal to most readers capable of having an independent opinion and clearing their minds of cant.

From the figures as to the receipts which are published it appears that a full chance of recording its opinion was scarcely given the public. On this point I am not prepared to speak. Such rebuff as the play encountered was, I fear, due to the preconceived attitude of some representatives of public opinion rather than to any misunderstanding between Mr. Jones and the public. Mr. Forbes Robertson's performance of the hero was superb in all respects. The refusal of the part of the heroine by Mrs. Patrick Campbell, its destined exponent, was so far a calamity that it fostered the belief that there was something immoral in the part. In other respects I cannot regard the substitution for that actress of Miss Marion Terry as a misfortune.

JOSEPH KNIGHT.

LONDON, 12th February, 1896.

AUTHOR'S NOTE

THIS play was produced at the Lyceum Theatre on the 15th January, 1896, and was withdrawn on the 25th, the management suddenly announcing the last three nights in the morning papers of the 23d. An impression has therefore prevailed in the public mind that the piece was a great financial failure. So far was this from being the case that the receipts for the first ten nights during which it was played were more than £100 higher than the receipts for the first ten nights of my play "The Middleman," which proved so great a financial success in England and America. The takings during the brief run at the Lyceum were as follows:—

January 15.	£209	7s.	6d.	January 21.	£ 99	9s.	11d.
" 16.	128	9	3	" 22.	114	14	4
" 17.	123	12	3	" 23.	121	18	0
" 18.	203	5	5	" 24.	146	12	7
" 20.	99	9	4	" 25.	231	7	0

The great number of sympathetic letters that I have received about the play and its cordial reception on the later nights of the run show that it created a deep impression on those who did see it, and encourage me to hope that I may introduce it again to the English public under happier auspices.

HENRY ARTHUR JONES.

PERSONS REPRESENTED.

THE REVEREND MICHAEL FEVERSHAM.
SIR LYOLF FEVERSHAM.
EDWARD LASHMAR (FATHER HILARY).
ANDREW GIBBARD.
THE REVEREND MARK DOCWRAY.
WITHYCOMBE.

AUDRIE LESDEN.
ROSE GIBBARD.
MRS. CANTELO.
FANNY CLOVER.

Villagers, Congregation, Choristers, Priests.

ACT I.

THE VICARAGE PARLOUR AT CLEVEHEDDON.

(*Four months pass.*)

ACT II.

THE SHRINE ON SAINT DECUMAN'S ISLAND.

(*Two nights and a day pass.*)

ACT III.

THE VICARAGE PARLOUR AS IN ACT I.

(*A year passes.*)

ACT IV.

THE MINSTER CHURCH AT CLEVEHEDDON.

(*Ten months pass.*)

ACT V.

RECEPTION ROOM OF THE MONASTERY OF SAN SALVATORE AT MAJANO, ITALY.

ACT I

SCENE.—*The Vicarage parlour at Cleveheddon. An old-fashioned comfortable room in an old English house. A large window, with low broad sill, takes up nearly all the back of the stage, showing to the right a part of Cleveheddon Minster in ruins. To the left a stretch of West Country landscape. A door, right, leading to house. A fireplace, right. A door, left. Table with chairs, right. A portrait of* MICHAEL'S *mother hangs on wall at a height of about nine feet. It is a very striking painting of a lady about twenty-eight, very delicate and spirituelle. Time.—A fine spring morning. Discover at the window, looking off right, with face turned away from audience, and in an attitude of strained attention to something outside,* ANDREW GIBBARD. *Enter* FANNY CLOVER, *the vicarage servant, showing in the* REVEREND MARK DOCWRAY, *a middle-aged clergyman.*

FANNY. Mr. Feversham is over to the church, sir, but he'll be back directly. (*Exit.*)

MARK. Andrew——

(ANDREW *turns round, an odd, rather seedy, carelessly-dressed man, a little over forty, rather gaunt, longish hair, an intelligent face with something slightly sinister about it. He shows signs of great recent sorrow and distress.*)

MARK. Andrew, what is it?
ANDR. I'd rather not tell you, Mr. Docwray.
MARK. Nothing has happened to Mr. Feversham?
ANDR. No.
MARK. Come! Come! What's the matter?
ANDR. My daughter——
MARK. What ails her? Where is she?
ANDR. Over at the church.
MARK. What is she doing?
ANDR. Making a public confession.
MARK. Public confession — of what?
ANDR. You'll be sure to hear all about it, so I may as well tell you myself. Perhaps it was my fault, perhaps I neglected her. All my time is given to Mr. Feversham in the library here. While I was buried in my work, and sometimes staying here half the night with Mr. Feversham, a scoundrel ruined my girl. Of course my only thought was to hide it. Was I wrong?

MARK. Go on. Tell me all.

ANDR. Well, right or wrong, I sent her away to the other end of England. Her child only lived a few weeks. And I brought her back home thinking it was all hushed up.

MARK. But it became known?

ANDR. Yes. Little by little, things began to leak out. Well, you may blame me if you like — I lied about it; and the more lies I told, the more I had to tell to cover them. Mr. Feversham heard of it and questioned us. Like a fool I lied to him. <u>It wasn't like lying, it was like murdering the truth to tell lies to him.</u> And she had to lie, too. Of course he believed us and defended us against everybody. And then we daredn't tell him the truth.

MARK. Go on. What else?

ANDR. There's nothing else. It all had to come out at last.

MARK. What did Mr. Feversham do?

ANDR. He persuaded us that we could never be right with ourselves, or right with our neighbours, or right with our God, till we had unsaid all our lies, and undone our deceit. So we've confessed it this morning.

MARK. In church? In public?

ANDR. Yes. I wouldn't have minded it for myself. But was it necessary for her — for Rose? Was it bound to be in public before all her companions, before all who had watched her grow up from a child?

MARK. You may be sure Mr. Feversham wouldn't have urged it unless he had felt it to be right and necessary.

ANDR. I wouldn't have done it for anybody else in

the world. I feel almost as if I were quits with him for all his favours to me.

MARK. You mustn't speak like this. Remember all he has done for you.

ANDR. Oh, I don't forget it. I don't forget that I was his scout's son, and that he educated me and made me his friend and companion and helper — there isn't a crumb I eat or a thread I wear that I don't owe to him. I don't forget it. But after this morning, I feel it isn't I who am in Mr. Feversham's debt — it's he who is in my debt.

(*A penitential hymn, with organ accompaniment, is sung in church outside.*)

ANDR. (*looking off*). It's over. They're coming out.

MARK. Why aren't you there, in church, by her side?

ANDR. I was. I went to church with her. I stood up first and answered all his questions, and then I stood aside, and it was her turn. I saw her step forward, and I noticed a little twitch of her lip like her mother used to have, and then — I couldn't bear it any longer — I came away. I know it was cowardly, but I couldn't stay. (*Looking off.*) Hark! They're coming! She's coming with the sister who is going to take her away.

MARK. Take her away?

ANDR. Mr. Feversham thinks it better for her to be away from the gossip of the village, so he has found a home for her with some sisters in London. She's going straight off there. Perhaps it's best. I don't know.

> (ROSE GIBBARD, *sobbing, with her face in her hands, passes the window from right to left, supported by an Anglican sister. The* REVEREND MICHAEL FEVERSHAM *follows them and passes window. A crowd of villagers come up to the window and look in. A moment or two later,* ROSE GIBBARD *enters left, supported by the sister.* ROSE *is a pretty delicate girl of about twenty, with rather refined features and bearing.*)

ANDR. (*holding out his arms to her*). Bear up, my dear. Don't cry! It breaks my heart to see you.

> *Enter the* REVEREND MICHAEL FEVERSHAM, *about forty; pale, strong, calm, ascetic, scholarly face, with much sweetness and spirituality of expression; very dignified, gentle manners, calm, strong, persuasive voice, rarely raised above an ordinary speaking tone. His whole presence and bearing denote great strength of character, great dignity, great gentleness, and great self-control.*
>
> *The villagers gather round the outside of the window and look in with mingled curiosity, rudeness, and respect.* MICHAEL *goes up to left window, opens it. The villagers draw back a little.*

MICH. (*speaking in a very calm voice*). Those of you who are filled with idle foolish curiosity, come and look in. (*They fall back.*) Those of you who have been moved by the awful lesson of this morning, go to your homes, ponder it in your hearts, so that all your actions and all your thoughts from this time forth may be as open as the day, as clear as crystal, as white as snow.

(*They all go away gradually.* MICHAEL *comes away from the window, leaving it open, goes to* MARK.)

MICH. Mark! (*Cordial handshake.*) You've come to stay, I hope?

MARK. A few days. You have a little business here? (*Glancing at the group of* ROSE, ANDREW, *and* Sister.)

MICH. It's nearly finished. Leave me with them for a few moments.

MARK. I'll get rid of the dust of my journey and come back to you.

(*Exit* MARK. MICHAEL *turns towards* ROSE *with great tenderness.*)

MICH. Poor child!

(*She comes towards him with evident effort; the* Sister *brings a chair and she sinks into it, sobbing.*)

MICH. (*bending over her with great tenderness*). I know what you have suffered this morning. I would willingly have borne it for you, but that would not have made reparation to those whom you have deceived, or given you peace in your own soul. (*She continues sobbing.*) Hush! Hush! All the bitterness is past! Look only to the future! Think of the happy newness and whiteness of your life from this moment! Think of the delight of waking in the morning and knowing that you have nothing to hide! Be sure you have done right to own your sin. There won't be a softer pillow in England to-night than the one your head rests upon. (*She becomes quieter.* MICHAEL *turns to the* Sister.) Watch over her very carefully. Keep her from brooding. Let her be occupied constantly with work. And write to me very often to tell me how she is. (*Turns to* ROSE.) The carriage is ready. It's time to say good-bye.

ROSE. Good-bye, sir. Thank you for all your kindness. I've been very wicked ——

MICH. Hush! That is all buried now.

ROSE. Good-bye, father.

> (*Throws her arms round* ANDREW'S *neck, clings to him, sobs convulsively for some moments in a paroxysm of grief.* MICHAEL *watches them for some moments.*)

MICH. (*intercepts, gently separates them*). It's more than she can bear. Say good-bye, and let her go.

ANDR. (*breaking down*). Good-bye, my dear! (*Kissing her.*) Good-bye — I — I — I ——

> (*Tears himself away, goes up to window, stands back to audience.*)

MICH. (*To* ROSE.) No more tears! Tears are for evil and sin, and yours are all past! Write to me and tell me how you get on, and how you like the work. It will bring you great peace — great peace. Why, you are comforted already — I think I see one of your old happy smiles coming. What do you think, sister, isn't that the beginning of a smile?

SISTER. Yes, sir. I think it is.

ROSE. Good-bye, sir — thank you for all your goodness. I — I —— (*Beginning to sob again.*)

MICH. No, no, you are forgetting. I must see a little smile before you go. Look, Andrew. (ANDREW *turns round.*) For your father's sake. When you have gone you will like him to remember that the last time he saw your face it wore a smile. That's brave! Good-bye! Good-bye!

> (ROSE *with great effort forces a smile and goes off with the* Sister. *A moment or two later she is seen to pass the window sobbing in the* Sister's *arms.*)

ANDR. Look! Oh, sir, was it bound to be in public, before everybody who knew her?

MICH. Believe me, Andrew, if my own sister, if my own child had been in your daughter's place, I would have counselled her to act as your daughter has done.

ANDR. She'll never hold up her head again.

MICH. Would you rather that she held up her

head in deceit and defiance, or that she held it down in grief and penitence? Think what you and she have endured this last year, the deceit, the agony, the shame, the guilt!

ANDR. I can't think of anything except her standing up in the church. I shall never forget it.

MICH. Tell me you know I would willingly have spared you and her if it had been possible.

ANDR. Then it wasn't possible?

MICH. I have done to you this morning as I would wish to be done by if I had followed a course of continued deception.

ANDR. Ah, sir, it's easy for you to talk. You aren't likely to be tempted, so you aren't likely to fall.

MICH. I trust not! I pray God to keep me. But if ever I did, I should think him my true friend who made me confess and rid my soul of my guilt. And you think me your true friend, don't you, Andrew? (*Holding out hand.*) Won't you shake hands with me?

(ANDREW *takes* MICHAEL'S *hand reluctantly, shakes it half-heartedly; is going off at door.*)

MICH. (*calls*). Andrew, it will be very lonely in your own house now your daughter has gone. Come and live with me here. There is the large visitors' room. Take it for your own, and make this your home. You will be nearer to our work, and you will be nearer to me, my friend.

MARK *enters.*

MARK (*at door*). Am I interrupting?

MICH. No. Come in. My little talk with Andrew is finished. (*To* ANDREW.) Say you know I have done what is right and best for you and her.

ANDR. You've done what you thought was best for us, sir. I've never doubted that. I can't see anything straight or clear this morning. (*Exit.*)

MARK. You've had a painful business here?

MICH. Terrible! But I was bound to go through with it. The whole village was talking of it. I believed in her innocence and defended her to the last. So when the truth came out I daren't hush it up. I should have been accused of hiding sin in my own household. But that poor child! My heart bled for her! Don't let us speak any more of it. Tell me about yourself and the work in London.

MARK. You must come and join us there.

(MICHAEL *shakes his head.*)

MICH. I couldn't live there. Every time I go up for a day or two I come back more and more sickened and frightened and disheartened. Besides, you forget my Eastern studies. They are my real work. I couldn't pursue them in the hurry and fever of London.

MARK. How are you getting on with the Arabic translations?

MICH. Slowly but surely. Andrew is invaluable to

me. In spite of his bringing up, he has the true instincts of the scholar.

MARK. Well, you know best. But we want you in London. You'd soon raise the funds for restoring the Minster.

MICH. (*shakes his head*). I can't go round with the hat.

MARK. How's the work getting on?

MICH. Very slowly. I'm afraid I shall never live to finish it. By the bye, I received fifty pounds anonymously only yesterday.

MARK. Have you any idea where it came from?

MICH. No. The Bank advised me that it had been paid to my credit by a reader of my "Hidden Life," who desired to remain anonymous.

MARK. The book is having an enormous influence. Nothing else is talked about. And it has gained you one very rich proselyte — this Mrs. Lesden. She's living here, isn't she?

MICH. Yes. Curious woman ——

MARK. Have you seen much of her?

MICH. I called, of course. I've met her once or twice at dinner. She has called here three or four times, and wasted several good hours for me.

MARK. How wasted?

MICH. Kept me from my work. I wish the woman would take herself back to London.

MARK. Why?

MICH. Her frivolity and insincerity repel me. No

— not insincerity. I recall that. For she said one or two things that seemed to show a vein of true, deep feeling. But on the whole I dislike her — I think I dislike her very much.

MARK. Why?

MICH. She comes regularly to church ——

MARK. Surely there's no very great harm in that ——

MICH. No; but I don't know whether she's mocking, or criticising, or worshipping; or whether she's merely bored, and thinking that my surplice is not enough starched, or starched too much.

MARK. She's very rich, and would be an immense help to our movement. I should try and cultivate her.

MICH. I can't cultivate people. What do you think of her?

MARK. A very clever society woman, all the more clever that she was not born in society.

MICH. What do you know of her?

MARK. Merely what I wrote you in my letter. That she was the only daughter of an Australian millionaire. Her great-grandfather, I believe, was an Australian convict. She was sent to England to be educated, went back to Australia, married, lost her husband and father, came back to England a widow, took a house in Mayfair, entertained largely, gave largely to charities, read your book, "The Hidden Life," came down to see the country round here, made up her mind to live here, and wanted an introduction to you — which I gave her.

Enter FANNY, *announcing* SIR LYOLF FEVERSHAM, *an English country gentleman, about sixty-five, a little old-fashioned in manners and dress.   Exit* FANNY.

SIR LYOLF. Michael — Mr. Docwray! Glad to see you. You're talking business, or rather religion, which is your business. Am I in the way?

MICH. No, we're not talking business. We're discussing a woman.

SIR LYOLF. Aren't women nine-tenths of a parson's business? (MICHAEL *looks a little shocked.*) Excuse me, my dear boy. (*To* MARK.) I quite believe in all Michael is doing. I accept all his new doctrines, I'm prepared to go all lengths with him, on condition that I indulge the latent old Adam in me with an occasional mild joke at his expense. But (*with great feeling*) he knows how proud I am of him, and how thankful I am to God for having given me a son who is shaping religious thought throughout England to-day, and who (*with a change to sly humour*) will never be a bishop — not even an archdeacon — I don't believe he'll be so much as a rural dean. What about this woman you were discussing? I'll bet — (*coughs himself up*) — I should say, I'll wager — (MICHAEL *looks shocked,* SIR LYOLF *shrugs his shoulders at* MARK, *proceeds in a firm voice*) — without staking anything, I will wager I know who the lady is — Mrs. Lesden? Am I right?

MICH. Yes.

Sir Lyolf. Well, I haven't heard your opinion of her. But I'll give you mine — without prejudice — (*with emphasis*) very queer lot.

Mark. Michael had just said she was a curious creature.

Mich. I don't understand her.

Sir Lyolf. When you don't understand a woman, depend upon it there's something not quite right about her.

Mich. She seems to have immense possibilities of good and evil.

Sir Lyolf. Nonsense. There are all sorts of men, but, believe me, there are only two sorts of women — good and bad.

Mich. You can't divide women into two classes like that.

Sir Lyolf. But I do — sheep and goats. Sheep on the right hand — goats on the left.

Mich. (*shaking his head*). Women's characters have greater subtlety than you suppose.

Sir Lyolf. Subtlety is the big cant word of our age. Depend upon it, there's nothing in subtlety. It either means hair-splitting or it means downright evil. The devil was the first subtle character we meet with in history.

Mich. And he has still something to do with the shaping of character in this world.

Sir Lyolf. I don't doubt it. And I think he has very likely something to do with the shaping of Mrs. Lesden's.

MICH. Hasn't he something to do with the shaping of all our characters? Don't all our souls swing continually between heaven and hell?

SIR LYOLF. Well, the woman whose soul swings continually between heaven and hell is not the woman whom I would choose to sit at my fireside or take the head of my table. Though I don't say I wouldn't ask her to dinner occasionally. That reminds me, how long are you staying, Mr. Docwray?

MARK. Only till Friday.

SIR LYOLF. You'll dine with me to-morrow evening?

MARK. Delighted.

SIR LYOLF. You too, Michael. I'll ask the Standerwicks, and (*suddenly*) suppose I ask this lady?

MICH. Mrs. Lesden? I would rather you didn't.

SIR LYOLF. Why not? If her soul is swinging between heaven and hell, it would only be kind of you to give it a jog towards heaven.

MICH. Very well — ask her. But I would rather you didn't speak lightly of ——

SIR LYOLF. Of her soul?

MICH. Of anyone's soul?

SIR LYOLF. I won't — even of a woman's. But I wish they wouldn't swing about. Women's souls oughtn't to swing anywhere, except towards heaven. Ah, Michael, you must let me have my fling. Remember when I was a boy, religion was a very simple, easy-going affair. Parson — clerk — old three-decker pulpit — village choir. What a village choir! I suppose it was all wrong — but they were very comfortable old days.

Mich. Religion is not simple — or easy-going.

Sir Lyolf. No. Subtlety again. I want a plain "yes" or "no," a plain black or white, a plain right or wrong, and none of our teachers or preachers is prepared to give it to me. Oh dear! This world has grown too subtle for me! I'll step over to Island House and ask Mrs. Lesden to dinner to-morrow.

Mark. I'll come with you and pay my respects to her. You don't mind, Michael?

Mich. Not at all. I want to set Andrew to work at once to keep him from dwelling on his trouble.

Sir Lyolf. I didn't come to the church this morning. I felt it would be too painful. (*Glancing up at portrait.*) What would she have said about it?

Mich. I think she approves what I have done.

Sir Lyolf (*looks at portrait, sighs, turns away*). Come, Mr. Docwray. I can't say I like this Mrs. Lesden of yours — I wonder why I'm going to ask her to dinner. (*Exit.*)

Mark (*who has been looking intently at portrait*). What a wonderful portrait that is of your mother! It seems as if she were alive!

Mich. She is. (*Exit* Mark *after* Sir Lyolf.)

⨯ Mich. (*goes up steps, takes portrait into his hand*). Yes, I have acted faithfully to my people, have I not? Whisper to me that I have done right to restore to this wandering father and child the blessing of a transparent life, a life without secrecy and without guile! Whisper to me that in this morning's work I have done what is well pleasing to my God and to you.

AUDRIE LESDEN, *about thirty, in a very fashionable morning dress, enters at back of window in the opposite direction to that in which* SIR LYOLF *and* MARK *have gone off. At first she seems to be watching them off. When she gets to the open window, she turns and sees* MICHAEL *with the portrait in his hand.* MICHAEL *very reverently kisses the portrait and places it on table; as he does so he sees her.*

MICH. Mrs. Lesden!
AUDR. Wasn't that Sir Lyolf who just went out?
MICH. Yes. I'll call him back——
AUDR. Please don't.
MICH. But he wishes to speak to you.
AUDR. I don't wish to speak to him.
MICH. Why not?
AUDR. I wish to speak to you.
MICH. About what?
AUDR. About my soul, about your soul, and about other people's souls. (*Leaning a little in at the window. He remains silent, and reserved. All through the early part of the scene his demeanour is cold, constrained, and a little impatient. A pause.*) I know

you make it a rule always to see people about their souls.

MICH. (*very coldly*). If they are really in need of spiritual advice.

AUDR. I think I'm in need of spiritual advice. (*A pause. He stands cold, irresponsive.*) Did you see me in church?

MICH. Yes.

AUDR. The whole thing was delightfully novel. (*He frowns.*) Do you mean to repeat this morning's scene?

MICH. Scene?

AUDR. It was a " scene," you know. I felt terribly distressed for the poor girl. And yet I envied her.

MICH. Envied her?

AUDR. (*leaning a little more in at the window*). You must allow she was the heroine of the occasion, though you were certainly very impressive yourself, and did your part very well. Still, after all, it's the man who is to be hanged who is the central figure in the proceedings. And the poor little creature looked exquisitely pathetic and graceful, and so sweetly innocent — quite good enough to go to heaven right away, I thought. A Sunday-school teacher told me once that it is nearly always the good girls who are betrayed. Is that so?

MICH. (*coldly*). You came to speak to me about yourself.

AUDR. So I did. Do you know when I saw that

girl standing there and looking so interesting, I felt I wouldn't mind making a public confession myself — if you thought it would benefit the parish — and if you would allow me to wear a special dress for the occasion?

(MICHAEL *turns round quickly as if about to speak angrily to her, stops, remains silent.*)

AUDR. (*musingly*). I suppose one couldn't confess in anything except black or white. It couldn't be done in red or yellow — or blue. Pale grey might do. (*Pause.*) What do you think?

(MICHAEL *does not reply.*)

AUDR. (*leaning a little more in at the window, in a much lower and subtler tone*). Don't you find it an exquisite pleasure to feel your sense of power over your people, especially over us poor women?

MICH. When you come to me you are neither man nor woman — you are only a soul in sin and distress.

AUDR. Oh, no! I won't be an "it." I insist on being a woman, though I don't mind *having* a soul — and in sin and distress, too. And I would save it — only I always think it's such a selfish piece of business, saving one's soul, — don't you? — so unkind to all one's neighbours? (*He stands half-bored, half-angry. A little pause.*) Do you know what I was thinking in church this morning?

MICH. No.

AUDR. I was comparing the delights of three different professions, — the soldier's, the doctor's, and the priest's. What a glorious joy it must be to ride to meet a man who is riding to kill you — *and to kill him!* But I'd rather be a doctor, and play with life and death. To have a man in your power, to see him lying tossing on his bed, and to think, "This may cure him, or it may kill him. Shall I risk it? At any rate, if he dies, I shall have learnt so much. I will risk it! And — he dies — No, he lives! I've saved him." Wouldn't you like to be a doctor?

MICH. No.

AUDR. That's because you know what far greater joy it is to be a priest. (*He turns very angrily.*) To play with people's souls ——

MICH. Play!

AUDR. You do play with our souls, don't you? They're in your hands. To think, "This man, or, say, this woman, has an immortal soul. She is vain, silly, deceitful, foolish, perhaps wicked, perhaps horribly wicked. She'll lose her soul and be eternally lost. But if I were to struggle with her for it, rebuke her, teach her, plead with her, entreat her, guide her — who knows — she's not wholly bad — I might save her? Is she worth saving? The worse she is, the greater will be my reward and honour for having saved her. Shall I do it? This woman's soul is in my keeping! I can choose for her eternal life or eternal death. What shall I do? Shall I save her, or let her be lost?"

MICH. (*comes eagerly to the window*). Do you mean that?

AUDR. Mean what?

MICH. That your soul is in my keeping?

AUDR. Not at all. I meant nothing except that thoughts like these must constantly stray through a priest's mind. Don't they? (*Long pause.*) Why don't you speak?

MICH. (*cold, stern*). I have nothing to say.

(*Pause.*)

AUDR. (*taking out purse, taking out two notes*). Oh! I was forgetting — I've brought you a little contribution for the restoration of your Minster.

(*Putting notes on window-sill.* MICHAEL *stands cold, angry.*)

AUDR. Won't you take it?

MICH. Thank you. No.

AUDR. I think you're a little rude to me. I came as a heart-stricken penitent; you wouldn't accept me in that character. Then I came as a pious donor. You wouldn't accept me in that. You've kept me outside here — you haven't even asked me in.

MICH. (*very sternly*). Come in! (*She looks up, uncertain as to his intentions.*) (*Same cold, stern voice.*) Please to come in. That way — the outer door is open.

(*She goes off, he goes to door left, opens it, she comes in.*)

MICH. (*the moment she has entered closes door decisively, then turns round on her very sternly*). What brings you to this village, to my church, to my house? Why are you here? Come to me as a penitent, and I will try to give you peace! Come to me as a woman of the world, and I will tell you "The friendship of the world is enmity with God." It always has been so, it always will be. The Church has no need of you, of your pretended devotions, of your gifts, of your presence at her services. Go your way back to the world, and leave her alone." But you come neither as a penitent, nor as a woman of the world. You come like — like some bad angel, to mock, and hint, and question, and suggest. How dare you play with sacred things? How dare you?!

AUDR. (*very low, quiet, amused voice*). I do not think it seemly or becoming in a clergyman to give way to temper. If anyone had asked me I should have said it was impossible in you.

(*He stands stern, cold, repellent.*)

Enter ANDREW.

MICH. What is it, Andrew?
ANDR. I thought you were disengaged. (*Going.*)
MICH. So I am. I'll come to you at once.
(*Exit* ANDREW.)

MICH. (*to* AUDRIE). You are right. It is unseemly to give way to temper, and perhaps you won't think me rude if I guard myself against it in future by asking you not to call upon me until I can be of real service to you. Good morning.

AUDR. Mr. Feversham, Mr. Feversham. (MICHAEL *turns.*) I've been very rude and troublesome. I beg your pardon. Please forgive me.

MICH. Certainly. Pray say no more.

AUDR. I saw you kissing that portrait as I stood at the window. It is your mother?

MICH. Yes.

AUDR. What a good woman she must have been! Don't think because I am bad ——

MICH. Are you bad?

AUDR. Didn't you say I was? I don't know whether I'm bad or good, but I know that no woman longs to be good more than I do — sometimes.

MICH. Do you indeed?

AUDR. (*impulsively*). Let me kiss that portrait!
(*Leaning forward to do it.*)

MICH. (*peremptorily*). No.
(*Intercepts and stops her.*)

AUDR. Why not?

MICH. I'd rather you didn't.

AUDR. You don't think I'm good enough.

MICH. I cannot allow you.

AUDR. Who painted it?

MICH. A young Italian. My mother's brother is a Catholic priest, and at that time he was living at Rome. My mother went there for her health when I was three years old. This young Italian saw her and asked permission to paint her. She came home and died of consumption. Then my uncle sent this portrait to my father with the news that the young painter had also died of consumption.

AUDR. How strange! And you've had it ever since?

MICH. I was only a child when it came. I fell into the habit of saying my prayers before it. So when I first left home my father gave it to me; it has been with me ever since, at Eton, and Oxford, and in my different curacies.

AUDR. Won't you let me kiss it before I go?
(*Leaning towards it.*)

MICH. (*preventing her*). I'd rather you did not.

AUDR. Why not?

MICH. I have a strange belief about that picture. I'll hang it up.

AUDR. (*a little intercepting him*). No. Let me look at it. Let me hold it in my hands. I won't kiss it without your permission. (*She takes it and looks at it intently.*) Tell me — what is your strange belief about it?

MICH. My mother was a deeply religious woman, and before my birth she consecrated me to this service as Hannah consecrated Samuel. When she was dying she said to me, "I'm not leaving you. I shall watch over you every moment of your life. There's not a word, or a deed, or a thought of yours but I shall know it. You won't see me, but I shall be very near you. Sometimes my hands will be upon your head, but you won't know it; sometimes my arms will be round you, but you won't feel them; sometimes my lips will be on your face, but you won't know that I have kissed you. Remember you are watched by the dead."

AUDR. And you believe that you are watched by the dead?

MICH. Yes.

AUDR. And that she is with us now — in this room?

MICH. Yes.

AUDR. She is your good angel.

MICH. She is my good angel.

AUDR. I can understand why you did not wish me to kiss her.

(MICHAEL *makes a movement to take the picture.*)

AUDR. (*retains it*). No. Yes, I feel she must be in this room.

MICH. Why?

AUDR. I was full of silly wicked thoughts when I came — she has taken them away.

MICH. Ah, if I dared hope that you would really change!

AUDR. Perhaps I will. (*Very imploringly.*) Do let me kiss this sweet face. (*Pause.*)

MICH. No — at least not now, not yet. Please give it back to me. (*He takes it.*) I'll hang it up. (*He takes it to steps.*) Will you hold it for a moment?

(*She comes to steps, holds it while he mounts, gives it to him.*)

AUDR. What a wonderful thought that is, that we are watched by the dead. It never occurred to me before. I wonder what a spirit is like? (*He hangs up the picture.*) Now she is quite out of my reach. (*He comes down steps.*) Won't you take that money for rebuilding the Minster! It's there on the window-sill. (*He goes and takes it.*) Thank you.

MICH. Thank you.

AUDR. Then I'm not to call again? Not even about my soul?

MICH. I'm going over to the Island for some time, and shall only be back on Sundays.

AUDR. Saint Decuman's Island. You've built yourself a house over there, haven't you?

MICH. The shrine was neglected and decayed. I restored it and built myself a couple of rooms round it. I've a few books, and just food and drink. I go over there sometimes for work and meditation.

AUDR. And yours is the only house on the island?

MICH. Yes.

AUDR. Isn't it awfully lonely there?

MICH. (*glancing at picture*). I'm never alone.

AUDR. No, you have your millions and millions of good and bad angels, besides hundreds of cheap excursionists.

MICH. Yes, in the summer, but they only stay a few hours.

AUDR. I can see the smoke from your chimney quite plainly in the evening from my drawing-room windows. How far is it across?

MICH. About four miles.

AUDR. I shall get Hannaford to row me over some day. Don't look alarmed. I won't come when you are there. I should frighten all your good angels away. (MICHAEL *shows a little impatience.*) You want to get rid of me. (*Going, suddenly turns.*) If I come to you as a penitent, you won't send me away?

MICH. Not if I can be of service to you.

AUDR. I seem to have changed my nature since I came into this room.

MICH. How?

AUDR. I don't know. I wonder how many natures I have and how often I can change them.

MICH. I wish you wouldn't speak like that.

AUDR. I won't. (*Very seriously.*) You said just now that I was playing with sacred things. I am, or I was until you spoke about her. (*With warning.*) Don't let me play with your soul.

MICH. I don't understand you.

AUDR. You may do me good, but I am far more likely to do you harm.

MICH. How?

AUDR. I'm not nearly so good a woman as you are a man.

MICH. But perhaps I may influence you for good.

AUDR. Do you think that you can have any influence on my soul without my having an equal influence on yours?

MICH. Action and re-action are equal and opposite. You think that law prevails in the spiritual world as well as in the material world?

AUDR. I'm sure it does. So let me go.

MICH. (*suddenly, with great feeling*). Oh, if I could save you!

AUDR. You can if you will. I would try so hard if you would only help me. But you don't believe that I can.

MICH. What makes you say that?

AUDR. You called me a bad angel — and you don't think me good enough to kiss her. (*Sidling up to the steps; he makes a deprecating movement to prevent her, but she takes no notice.*) If you knew it would give me a splendid impulse to goodness, would you refuse me? (*She watches him very closely; he watches her, half deprecating, half consenting; she goes up a step or two; he again makes a deprecating gesture, but does not stop her.*) Can't you see what an awful effect it would have on me if you thought me worthy to be in the company of your good angel? It would be almost a sacrament! (*Going up steps. He makes a stronger gesture of deprecation.*) Ah, you think I'm not worthy——

MICH. No, no——

AUDR. (*on top of steps, very seductively*). Do save me. I'm worth saving. (*Whispers.*) I may kiss her? I may? I may? (*He does not reply. She very reverently kisses the picture on the wall, turns round, comes down slowly to him.*) Your bad angel has kissed your good angel. (*A mock curtsey to him.*)

(*Exit softly.* MICHAEL *stands troubled.*)

CURTAIN.

(*Four months pass between Acts I. and II.*)

ACT II

SCENE.—*The Shrine on Saint Decuman's Island in the Bristol Channel. A living room built round the shrine of the Saint, a fine piece of decayed Decorated Gothic now in the back wall of the room. A large fireplace down right. A door above fireplace. A door left; two windows, one on each side of the shrine, show the sea with the horizon line and the sky above. A bookcase; a table; old oaken panelling, about seven feet high, all round the room, and above them white-washed walls. Red brick floor. Everything very rude and simple, and yet tasteful, as if it had been done by the village mason and carpenter under* MICHAEL'S *direction. Time, a September evening. Discover* ANDREW GIBBARD *packing a portmanteau, and* EDWARD LASHMAR (FATHER HILARY), *a Catholic priest, about sixty, very dignified and refined. Enter* WITHYCOMBE, *an old boatman.*

WITHY. Now, gentlemen, if yu'me ready to start! If yu daunt come sune, us shall lose the tide down.

FATHER H. I'm quite ready, Withycombe, as soon as I have said "Good-bye" to Mr. Feversham.

WITHY. Mr. Feversham ain't coming along with us, then?

ANDR. No, he stays on the island all the week, and you are to fetch him on Saturday morning.

WITHY. Saturday morning. To-day's Wednesday. Right you are. Well and good. Saturday morning. Yu'me coming on to Saint Margaret's along with us, Mr. Gibbard?

ANDR. Yes — we can find some accommodation there for the night, can't we?

WITHY. Well, I warn ye 'tis rough.

FATHER H. Rougher than my Master had on his first coming here?

WITHY. Well, I waun't say that, but so fur as I can judge 'tis about as rough.

FATHER H. Then it will do for me. Where is Mr. Feversham?

WITHY. A few minutes agone he wor watching the excursion steamer back to Lowburnham.

FATHER H. Will you find him and tell him that I am waiting to start?

WITHY. Right you are, sir. Well and good.
                                                   (*Exit.*)

FATHER H. Andrew — have you noticed any change in Mr. Feversham lately?

ANDR. Change, Father?

FATHER H. He seems so restless and disturbed, so unlike himself.

ANDR. Does he?

FATHER H. It's six years since I was in England. But he was always so calm and concentrated. Has he any trouble, do you know?

ANDR. He hasn't spoken of any.

FATHER H. No. But you're with him constantly. Surely you must have seen the difference in him?

ANDR. Yes. He is changed.

FATHER H. How long has he been like this?

ANDR. The last four months.

FATHER H. Do you know of any reason for it?

ANDR. He's coming!

Enter MICHAEL.

MICH. You're ready to start, Uncle Ned?

FATHER H. Yes. You won't change your mind and come with us?

MICH. No, I must stay here. (*Glancing at books, restlessly.*) I want to be alone. I couldn't be of any service to you over at Saint Margaret's?

FATHER H. There is the legend that connects her with Saint Decuman — I suppose no more is to be learnt of that than we already know?

MICH. No. The fisher people only know what they have learnt from the guide books.

ANDR. (*standing with portmanteau*). Have you anything more to take to the boat, Father?

FATHER H. No, that's all, Andrew.

ANDR. Then I'll take it down and wait for you there.   (*Exit* ANDREW *with portmanteau.*)

FATHER H. Then this is good-bye, Michael?

MICH. Unless you'll stay over the Sunday at Cleveheddon?

FATHER H. No, I've done my work in England, and I must be back among my people. I wanted to see the shrines on these two sister islands again before I died. I shall leave Saint Margaret's to-morrow morning, get back to Cleveheddon, take the afternoon train up to London, and leave for Italy on Friday morning. You'll come and see me at Majano?

MICH. When I can.

FATHER H. This winter?

MICH. No, not this winter. I shall be at work at once on the restorations now I've got all the money.

FATHER H. Strange that it should all come so soon within two or three months.

MICH. Yes, and from such different quarters of England — a thousand one day from Manchester — five hundred the next from some unheard-of village — and then the last great final gift last week.

FATHER H. It looks as if it all came from one giver?

MICH. Yes, I had thought that.

FATHER H. You don't know of any one?

MICH. I've one or two suspicions. However, the great fact is that I have it all, and can set my architects to work.

FATHER H. Michael — I was asking Andrew just now, there is something troubling you?

D

MICH. No — no. What makes you think that?

FATHER H. You are not yourself. (*Pause.*) Is it anything where I can be of help?

MICH. There is nothing. (*Pause.*) There has been something. But it is past. (FATHER HILARY *looks grave.*) You need have no fear for me.
(*Holding out hand.*)

FATHER H. (*takes his hand, holds it for a long while, looks gravely at him*). If you should ever need a deeper peace than you can find within or around you, come to me in Italy.

MICH. But I am at peace now. (*Restlessly, pushing his hand through hair, then a little querulously.*) I am at peace now. (FATHER HILARY *shakes his head.*) You think you can give me that deeper peace?

FATHER H. I know I can.

MICH. I may come to you some day.

(WITHYCOMBE *puts his head in at door.*)

WITHY. Now, sir, if yu plaise, we'me losing the tide — us shan't get to Margaret's avore supper-time.

FATHER H. I'm coming, Withycombe.

MICH. Withycombe, you'll come and fetch me on Saturday morning.

WITHY. Saturday morning, twelve o'clock sharp, I'm here. Right you are, Mr. Feversham. Well and good. (*Exit.*)

FATHER H. Good-bye.

MICH. Good-bye, Uncle Ned.

ACT II MICHAEL AND HIS LOST ANGEL 35

(*Very hearty hand-shake. Exit* FATHER HILARY.
MICHAEL *goes to door, stands looking a few
seconds, comes in, turns to his books.*)

Re-enter FATHER HILARY.

MICH. What is it?
FATHER H. I don't like leaving you. Come with
me to-night to Margaret's.
MICH. Shall I? Perhaps it would be best. Wait
a minute.
WITHY. (*voice heard of*). Now, Mr. Lashmar, if
you plaise, sir — we'me losing the tide.
MICH. Don't wait, I'm safe here. Good-bye.
FATHER H. (*slowly and regretfully*). Good-bye.

(*Exit slowly.* MICHAEL *watches* FATHER HILARY
*off; stays at door for some time, waves his
hand, then closes door.*)

MICH. Now I shall be at peace! (*Takes out letter
from his pocket.*) Her letter! I will not read it!
(*Puts it back in pocket, kneels and lights the fire.*)
Why did you come into my life? I did not seek
you! You came unbidden, and before I was aware
of it you had unlocked the holiest places of my heart.
Your skirts have swept through all the gateways of my
being. There is a fragrance of you in every cranny
of me. You possess me! (*Rises.*) No! No!
No! I will not yield to you! (*Takes up book, seats
himself at fire, reads a moment or two.*) You are
there in the fire! Your image plays in the shadows

— Oh, my light and my fire, will you burn me up with love for you? (*Rises, sighs.*) I'm mad! (*Pause, very resolutely.*) I will be master of myself — I will be servant to none save my work and my God! (*Seats himself resolutely, reads a moment or two, then drops book on knees.*) The wind that blows round here may perhaps play round her brow, the very breath that met my lips as I stood at the door may meet hers on the shore yonder. (*Rises, flings book on table, goes to window; takes out letter again, holds it undecidedly.*) Why shouldn't I read it? Every stroke of it is graven on my heart. — (*Opens it.*) "Dear keeper of souls in this parish, I have thought so much of our talk last night. I'm inclined to think that I have a soul after all, but it is a most uncomfortable possession. I believe if someone gave me an enormous impulse I might make a saint or a martyr, or anything that's divine. And I believe there is one man living who could give me that impulse." "One man living who could give me that impulse — " "But I hope he won't. Frankly, you may save me at too great cost to yourself. So trouble yourself no further about me. But if after this, you still think my wandering, dangling soul worth a moment of your ghostly care, come and lunch with me to-morrow, and I will give you the sweet plain butter-cakes that you love, on the old blue china. And that our salvation may not be too easy, I will tempt you with one sip of the ancient Johannisburg." And I went — yes, I went. "But for your own sake — I speak with all a woman's care for your earthly and heavenly welfare — I would rather you did not come. Let it be so. Let this be farewell. Perhaps our souls may salute each other in aimless vacancy hereafter, and I will smile as sweet a smile as I can without lips or cheeks to smile with, when I remember as I pass you in the shades that I saved you from your bad angel, Audrie Lesden. P.S. Be wise, and let me go." I cannot! I cannot! Yet if I do not — what remains for me? Torture, hopeless love, neglected duty, work cast aside and spoilt, all my life disordered and wrecked. Oh, if I could be wise — I will! I will tear out this last one dear sweet thought of her. (*Goes to fire, tears up the letter in little pieces, watches them burn.*) It's done! I've conquered! Now I shall be at peace.

>(*Sits himself resolutely at table, reads. A little tap at the door, he shows surprise; the tap is repeated, he rises, goes to door, opens it. At that moment* AUDRIE'S *face appears at the right-hand window for a moment. He looks out, stays there a moment or two, closes door, seats himself again at table, reads. The tap is repeated; he rises,* AUDRIE *appears at door, he shows a moment of intense delight which he quickly subdues.*)

AUDR. May I come in? (*Pause.*) You are busy — I'll go —

MICH. No — (*She stops on threshold.*) Come in.

She enters. He stands motionless at table. Sunset without. It gradually grows darker.

MICH. What brings you here?

AUDR. You did not expect me. You aren't accustomed to entertain angels unawares — even bad ones.

MICH. (*his voice thick and a little hoarse*). Your boat, your companions?

AUDR. I have no boat, and no companions.

MICH. (*horrified, delighted*). You're alone?

AUDR. Quite alone.

MICH. How did you come here?

AUDR. By the simplest and most prosaic means in the world. This morning I took the train to Lowburnham to do some shopping. As I was coming back to the station, a boy put this little handbill into my hand. (*Showing a little yellow handbill.*) Afternoon excursion to Saint Decuman's and Saint Margaret's Isles. I had an impulse — I obeyed it. I telegraphed to Cleveheddon for a boat to meet me here at six — (*takes out watch*) — it only wants ten minutes — and took the excursion steamer. They all landed here for half-an-hour. I hid myself till after the steamer had gone. Then I came up here to your cottage. I heard some voices, so I hid again — who was here?

MICH. Only my secretary and my uncle Ned.

AUDR. The Catholic priest. I saw a boat leaving — it was they?

Mich. Yes.
Audr. They're not coming back?
Mich. No.
Audr. You're annoyed with me for coming?
Mich. No, but wasn't it a little — imprudent?
Audr. Oh, I must do mad things sometimes, just to preserve my general balance of sanity. Besides, my boat will be here in ten minutes. (*Pause.*)
Audr. How strange we should be here alone!
Mich. The only two beings on this island — we two!
Audr. And our two souls.
Mich. I wish you wouldn't jest with sacred things.
Audr. I won't. (*Suddenly, impulsively.*) I want to be good! Help me to be good! You think I'm foolish and light and frivolous! Well, perhaps I am, but when I'm with you I'm capable of anything, anything — except being an ordinary, average, good woman.
Mich. But isn't that all that is required of a woman?
Audr. Perhaps. It's rather a damnable heritage, isn't it? And I'm not a barn-door fowl.
Mich. What are you?
Audr. Just what you like to make of me. Don't think I'm flattering you. Don't think I'm bold and unwomanly. I'm only speaking the truth. You have changed me. I'm ready to do anything, believe anything, suffer anything that you bid me! To-night I'm on a pinnacle! I shall either be snatched up to the

skies, or tumble into the abyss. Which will it be, I wonder?

MICH. (*after a struggle, in a calm voice*). Neither, I trust. I hope you will take your boat back in ten minutes, have a good passage across, a comfortable dinner from your pretty blue china, and a sound night's rest. And to-morrow you will wake and forget this rather imprudent freak.

AUDR. Oh, you won't tread the clouds with me! Very well! Down to the earth we come. I can be as earthly as the very clay itself. But I thought you wanted me to be spiritual.

MICH. I want you to be sincere, to be yourself.

AUDR. Very well. Tell me how. You are my ghostly father.

MICH. No, you've never allowed me to be a priest to you.

AUDR. I've never allowed you?

MICH. And I've never dared.

AUDR. Why not?

MICH. Because you've never allowed me to forget that I am a man.

AUDR. Very well. Don't be a priest to me — at least not now. Tell me some one thing that you would wish me to do, and I'll do it!

MICH. In that letter you wrote me ——

AUDR. Did you keep it?

MICH. No, I destroyed it.

AUDR. Destroyed it!

MICH. In that letter you said it would be better for us if we did not meet again ——

AUDR. No. I said it would be better for *you* if we did not meet again.

MICH. Better for me?

AUDR. Yes, and worse for me. I came here to-night to warn you ——

MICH. Against what?

AUDR. Myself. I've done something that may endanger your peace for ever.

MICH. What do you mean?

AUDR. Sometimes I laugh at it, sometimes I'm frightened. I daren't tell you what I've done. I'll go. (*Goes to door, opens it.*)

MICH. No. (*Stops her.*) Mrs. Lesden, what have you done against me? You don't mean your gifts to the Minster?

AUDR. My gifts — what gifts?

MICH. During the last four months I've constantly received large sums for the restoration of the Minster, and last week a very large sum was sent me, enough to carry out all the work just as I wished.

AUDR. Well?

MICH. It was you who sent it all.

AUDR. I must see if my boatman has come.

MICH. (*stopping her*). No. Why did you send the money — so many different sums from so many different places?

AUDR. Because that gave me dozens of pleasures

instead of one, in sending it. And I thought it would give you dozens of pleasures instead of one, in receiving it.

MICH. I knew it was you! How glad I am to owe it all to you! Words couldn't tell you how grateful I am.

AUDR. And yet you wouldn't walk the clouds with me for a few minutes?

MICH. You know that I would do anything in my power for your best, your heavenly welfare.

AUDR. I don't think I care much for my heavenly welfare just at this moment. You tumbled me off my pinnacle, and here I am stuck in the mud. (*Looking off at the open door.*) Look! That boat is half-way to Saint Margaret's.

MICH. Yes, they sleep there to-night.

AUDR. What a queer-looking man your secretary is. Is he quite trustworthy?

MICH. Quite. Why?

AUDR. I caught him looking at you in a very strange way a week or two back.

MICH. He's devoted to me.

AUDR. I'm glad of that. How far is it to Saint Margaret's?

MICH. Three miles.

AUDR. Do you believe the legend about Saint Decuman and Saint Margaret?

MICH. That they loved each other?

AUDR. Yes, on separate islands, and never met.

Mich. They denied themselves love here that they might gain heavenly happiness hereafter.

Audr. Now that their hearts have been dust all these hundreds of years, what good is it to them that they denied themselves love?

Mich. You think ——

Audr. I think a little love on this earth is worth a good many paradises hereafter. It's a cold world, hereafter. It chills me to the bone when I think of it! *(Shivers a little and comes away from the door.)* I'm getting a little cold.

Mich. *(placing chair)*. Sit by the fire.

(She sits near fire, which is blazing up; he goes and closes door.)

Audr. *(putting on some logs)*. Do I know you well enough to make your fire for you?

Mich. I hope so.

(She sits; he stands above her for some seconds, watching her keenly; a long pause.)

Audr. You were looking at me. What were you thinking of?

Mich. I was wondering what memories are stored in that white forehead.

Audr. Memories? *(Long sigh.)* A few bright ones, and many sad ones.

Mich. Your past life was not happy?

Audr. *(a little shudder of recollection)*. No. And yours? Tell me ——

Mich. What?

Audr. Something about your past life, something you've never told to a living creature.

Mich. When I was twenty——

Audr. Stay — what were you like when you were twenty? (*Shuts her eyes, puts her hand over them.*) Now I can see you when you were twenty.

Mich. Is there anyone with me?

Audr. No, I can't see her. What was she like? Fair or dark?

Mich. Fair, with changing grey eyes that could be serious or merry as she pleased, and fine clear features, and the sweetest provoking mouth——

Audr. I hate her. Who was she?

Mich. Miss Standerwick's niece. She stayed there all the summer that year.

Audr. Was that a happy summer?

Mich. The happiest I have ever known — till this.

Audr. Ah!

Mich. I used to go to evening church and follow them home, and wait outside till I could see the candle in her window. When it went out I used to walk home.

Audr. Across those fields where we walked the other night?

Mich. Yes.

Audr. I'll never walk that way again. Go on.

Mich. One night as I was waiting, she came out suddenly. I couldn't speak for trembling. At last I found my tongue, and we talked about silly commonplace things. When she was going in I dared to breathe, "Give me one kiss." She didn't answer. I just touched her cheek with my lips, and I whispered, "Good-night, Nelly." She said, "Good-night, Mike."

AUDR. She called you Mike?

MICH. I was called Mike when I was a boy.

AUDR. And your next meeting?

MICH. She was called away early the next morning to her father's deathbed. Her mother went abroad. I never saw her again. Tell me something about your past life.

AUDR. Can you see me when I was eight? I was a pretty little brown maid, and I set all aflame the heart of a cherub aged ten, with strong fat legs and curly red hair. His sister was my dearest friend. He spent all his pocket-money in buying sugar-plums for me, and gave them to her to give to me. She ate them herself, and slandered me to him, for she said I was false. He kicked her on the nose, and was sent far — far away to school. This was the first tragedy of my life. Now tell me some more of your life. You have had other romances, darker, deeper ones?

MICH. Nothing that I dare show. I have told you of the one love of my youth. And you —— Have you had darker, deeper romances?

AUDR. I was unhappy without romance. I would show you all my heart, all my thoughts, all my life, if I could do it as one shows a picture, and let it speak for itself. I wonder if you'd condemn me ——

MICH.   Condemn you!

AUDR.   I don't think you would. You have never guessed——

MICH.   Guessed——

AUDR.   What a world there is within oneself that one never dares speak of! I wish to hide nothing from you. I would have you know me through and through for just the woman that I am, just that and no other, because, don't you see — I don't want to cheat you of a farthing's-worth of esteem on false pretences — I want you to like me, Audrie Lesden, and not some myth of your imagination. But if you were armed with all the tortures of hell for plucking the truth about myself from my lips, I should still hide myself from you. So, guess, guess, guess, grand inquisitor — what is here (*tapping her forehead*) and here! (*Putting her hand on her heart.*) You'll never guess one thousandth part of the truth!

MICH.   But tell me something in your past life that you have never told to another creature.

AUDR.   I have two great secrets — one is about yourself, one is about another man.

MICH.   Myself? Another man?

AUDR.   My husband.

MICH.   You said you had been unhappy.

AUDR.   I married as thousands of girls do, carelessly, thoughtlessly. I was married for my money. No one had ever told me that love was sacred.

MICH. Nobody ever does tell us that, till we hear it from our own hearts.

AUDR. I suppose it was my own fault. I was very well punished.

MICH. How long were you married?

AUDR. Two years.

MICH. And then your husband died?

AUDR. He went away from me. I never saw him again — alive. (*Passionately.*) And there's an end of him!

MICH. I won't ask you what that secret is. I would wish you to keep it sacred. But your secret about myself? Surely I may ask that?

AUDR. I have sold you to the devil.

MICH. What?

AUDR. I have sold myself, too.

MICH. Still jesting?

AUDR. No, I did it in real, deep earnest.

MICH. I don't understand you.

AUDR. Six months ago I was tired, gnawn to the very heart with ennui, and one hot restless night I happened to take up your book, "The Hidden Life." It came to me — oh, like a breath of the purest, freshest air in a fevered room. I thought I should like to know you. I got up early, took the first morning train down here, looked about the place, saw the Island House was to let, and rented it for three years.

MICH. Well?

AUDR. I got Mr. Docwray to give me an introduction to you. You annoyed me, you were so cold and priestlike. Each time I saw you, you piqued and angered me more and more. I longed to get some power over you. At last one day after you had been so frozen and distant a little black imp jumped into my brain and whispered to me. I said to the devil, "Give this sculptured saint to me, and I'll give both our souls to you."

MICH. But you didn't mean it?

AUDR. Yes. I said it with all my heart, and I bit my arm — look — (*Showing her arm.*) I made the teeth meet. There's the mark. If there is a devil, he heard me.

MICH. And you think he has given me to you?

AUDR. The next time I saw you, you let me kiss your mother's portrait.

MICH. Ah!

AUDR. But you don't really believe there is a devil? Why don't you speak? Why don't you laugh at me and tell me it's all nonsense? I haven't really given the devil power over your soul?

MICH. No devil has any power over any soul of man until the man himself first gives him entrance and consent.

AUDR. And you haven't! Say you don't care for me.

MICH. How can I say that?

AUDR. You must! I'm not strong enough to leave you of my own free will. I shall hang about you, worry you, tease you, tempt you, and at last, destroy you. Don't let me do it! Beat me away from you, insult me, do something to make me hate you! Make me leave you!

MICH. When I love you with all my being?

AUDR. (*shows great delight*). And you dare go on? It's an awful delight to think that a man would dare to risk hell for one! There aren't many men who would dare lose this world for the woman they love — how many men are there that would dare to lose the other?

MICH. We must lose this world, for I am vowed away from all earthly things. But why should we lose the other? Why should we not make our love the lever to raise our souls? You do love me?

AUDR. Love is hardly the word. It is more like — if a man could create a dog, and be her master, friend, father, and God, I think she would feel towards him something of what I feel towards you. You have first made me know what love is, what life is. You have changed me thoroughly — no, you have changed half of me thoroughly — one half is still worthless, silly, capricious, hollow, worldly, and bad — that's my old self. She is gradually withering up under your influence, that old Audrie Lesden. The other half is looking out of my eyes at you now! Look! do you see the new Audrie Lesden that is your daughter and your creature? Aren't you proud of her?

MICH. I shall be proud of her when she is full

grown and dares to leave me of her own free will, because she loves me, and because I am vowed to Heaven!

AUDR. Do I tempt you? I'll go. You love me. That's enough, or it should be enough. I'll get back to London to-morrow, and strangle the new Audrie. Then the old Audrie will come back again, and live the old weary, dry, empty life — and grow old and wrinkled and heartless and perhaps — rouged ——

MICH. Why do you tear me so? What do you want of me here or hereafter? Take it! It's yours ——

AUDR. You dare go on — now you know?

MICH. Yes.

AUDR. Ah! I thought it was only women who dared hell for love. I won't take your sacrifice — I will leave you.

MICH. You will? Yes, it must be so! My work, my vows — I cannot, may not taste of earthly love. Oh, it's cruel to dash the cup from my lips! (*Pause; then very calmly.*) You are right! I feel that we are choosing heaven or hell for both our souls this night! Help me to choose heaven for you, and I'll help you to choose heaven for me.

AUDR. Good-bye, my love, for ever. Be brave — and very cold to me, now. Be like marble — and death.

MICH. (*takes her hand; a very long pause; then speaks very calmly*). It is victory, isn't it? We have conquered? I'll go down to the bay and see if your boat has come. (*By this time it is dark outside.*)

AUDR. Half-past six. I shall have a cold, dark voyage.

MICH. And it is just a little rough. But Hannaford is a careful boatman.

AUDR. It's not Hannaford who is coming for me. I telegraphed for Withycombe.

MICH. (*pause—very pale and cold*). Withycombe? But you always employ Hannaford?

AUDR. Yes; and I did write out one telegram to him, and then I thought I should like to go back in the boat that always takes you. So I tore up the telegram to Hannaford, and telegraphed to Withycombe.

MICH. Withycombe?

AUDR. Yes, what's the matter?

MICH. He lives alone. When he goes out, he locks up his cottage. Your telegram will wait at the post office.

AUDR. Why?

MICH. Withycombe has gone over to Saint Margaret's with Gibbard and my uncle. They stay there the night.

AUDR. Your own boat?

MICH. I had it towed back last week, so that I couldn't be tempted to come to you.

AUDR. Then——?

MICH. (*looks at her*). No boat will come to-night.

(*Looks at her more intently.*) No boat will come to-night!

(*They stand looking at each other.*)

VERY SLOW CURTAIN.

(*Two nights and a day — from Wednesday evening to Friday morning — pass between Acts II. and III.*)

ACT III

SCENE. — *The Vicarage parlour, as in first act. Morning. Enter* MICHAEL, *haggard, troubled, with self-absorbed expression, the expression of a man trying to realize that he has committed a great and irrevocable sin; he stands for some moments helpless, dreamy, as if unconscious of his whereabouts; then looks round; his eyes fall upon his mother's picture, he shudders a little, shows intense pain. At length he goes up the steps, takes the picture down, places it on the floor with its face against the wall, carefully avoiding all the while to look at it. He then moves to table in the same dreamy, helpless, self-absorbed state, sits, looks in front of him. Enter* ANDREW, *comes up behind him.*

MICH. Oh, Andrew —— Well?

ANDR. (*coming up to him*). I want to consult you on that passage in the Arabic — if you can spare the time.

MICH. Bring the manuscripts here. (MICHAEL *unconsciously looks at his hands.*) What are you looking at?

ANDR. Nothing. Your hands are blistered?

MICH. I did a little rowing — the other day. Bring the manuscripts. (ANDREW *goes to door.*)

MICH. Andrew — (ANDREW *stops*) — I was very restless — did you hear me stirring in the night?

ANDR. Stirring?

MICH. Yes, I couldn't sleep. I got up about one and went out — walked about for some hours — it was nearly light when I came in again. Did you hear me?

ANDR. (*pauses, then answers*). No.

(*Is about to go off at right door when* FANNY *enters left. He stops.*)

FANNY. Mrs. Lesden wishes to see you for a minute or two about one of her cottagers.

(ANDREW *watches* MICHAEL *keenly, but unobtrusively.*)

MICH. (*after a little start of surprise, in a tone of affected carelessness*). Show her in.

(*Exit* ANDREW, *right. Exit* FANNY, *left.* MICHAEL *rises, shows great perturbation, walks about, watches the door for her entrance.*)

Re-enter FANNY, *left, showing in* AUDRIE.

FANNY. Mrs. Lesden.

(*Exit* FANNY. MICHAEL *and* AUDRIE *stand looking at each other for some seconds; then he goes to her, takes her hand, kisses it with great reverence, motions her to a chair; she sits.*

He holds out to her the palms of his hands with a rueful smile, shows they are much blistered as if with rowing.)

AUDR. Poor hands!

MICH. I'm not used to rowing. (*Pause.*)

AUDR. I didn't thank you.

MICH. Thank me!

AUDR. (*pause*). Wasn't it a terrible voyage, terrible and delightful? But we ought to have been drowned together!

MICH. Oh, don't say that — in sin! To be lost in sin!

AUDR. I'd rather be lost with you than saved with anyone else.

MICH. You mustn't speak like this ——

AUDR. It won't be right, you know, unless we are lost or saved together, will it?

MICH. Hush! Hush! (*Pause.*)

AUDR. You're sorry?

MICH. No. And you?

AUDR. No. Is all safe, do you think?

MICH. Yes, I believe so.

AUDR. Didn't that strange secretary of yours think it curious that you came back on Thursday instead of Saturday?

MICH. No. I explained that when Withycombe brought me your telegram I thought it better to return at once in case you had started to come, and had been somehow lost.

AUDR. Let us go carefully through it all as it happened, to make sure. To-day is Friday. On Wednesday I telegraphed to Withycombe to be at the landing-place at Saint Decuman's with a boat at six o'clock in the evening to bring me back home from there.

MICH. Yes.

AUDR. But being a strange creature and quite unaccountable for my actions, I changed my mind, and instead of coming to Saint Decuman's I went up to London, stayed there all day yesterday, and returned by the night mail, reaching home at seven this morning.

MICH. Yes.

AUDR. Meantime Withycombe has gone to Saint Margaret's with your uncle, stays there Wednesday night and does not get my telegram till his return home yesterday afternoon. He consults my servants, who know nothing of my whereabouts, consults Mr. Gibbard, who advises him to go to Saint Decuman's and see if I am there. He reaches Saint Decuman's last evening. You are surprised when he shows you the telegram — you explain that I'm not there, that I haven't been there, that you've seen nothing of me. (*Very tenderly.*) Dear, I felt so sorry for you when I heard you blundering and stammering through your tale to Withycombe.

MICH. Why?

AUDR. I knew the pain and shame it caused you to say what wasn't true. I wished I could have told all the lies for you.

MICH. No, no. Isn't the truth dear to you?

AUDR. Not in comparison with you. Besides, I shall be let off my fibs and little sins very cheaply, much more cheaply than you'll be, great serious person.

MICH. You grieve me to the heart when you speak like this ——

AUDR. (*penitent*). I won't! I won't! I'll be very good and quite serious. Where were we? Well, you explain to Withycombe that I have never been to Saint Decuman's, and at the same time you also change your mind and return with him last evening instead of staying till Saturday.

MICH. You've seen Withycombe and told him you went to London?

AUDR. Yes.

MICH. He suspects nothing?

AUDR. No, I made it all quite clear to him.

MICH. And your servants?

AUDR. They're used to my absences. They think nothing of it.

MICH. Then all is safe. The matter will never be heard of again — except ——

AUDR. Except?

MICH. In our two hearts, and in the High Court where such cases are tried.

(*With an inclination of the head and finger towards heaven.*)

AUDR. Don't preach, and — don't regret.

MICH. I won't — only how strange it all is!

AUDR. What?

MICH. (*quiet, calm voice throughout, smiling a little*). How men try to make their religion square with their practice! I was hard, cruelly hard, on that poor little girl of Andrew's. I was sure it was for the good of her soul that she should stand up and confess in public. But now it comes to my own self, I make excuses; I hide, and cloak, and equivocate, and lie — what a hypocrite I am!

AUDR. Ah, you're sorry!

MICH. No, I'm strangely happy and — dazed. I feel nothing, except my great joy, and a curious bitter amusement in tracing it all out.

AUDR. Tracing what out?

MICH. The hundred little chances, accidents as we call them, that gave us to each other. Everything I did to avoid you threw me at your feet. I felt myself beginning to love you. I wrote urgently to Uncle Ned in Italy, thinking I'd tell him and that he would save me. He came — I couldn't tell him of you, but his coming kept Withycombe from getting your telegram. I went to Saint Decuman's to escape from you. You were moved to come to me. I sent away my own boat to put the sea between us; and so I imprisoned you with me. Six years ago I used all my influence to have the new lighthouse built on Saint Margaret's Isle instead of Saint Decuman's, so that I might keep Saint Decuman's lonely for myself and prayer. I kept it lonely for myself and *you*. It was what we call a chance I didn't go to Saint Margaret's with Andrew and my uncle. It was what we call a chance that you telegraphed to my boatman instead of your own. If any one thing had gone differently ——

AUDR. (*shaking her head*). We couldn't have missed each other in this world. It's no use blaming chance or fate, or whatever it is.

MICH. I blame nothing. I am too happy. Besides, Chance? Fate? I had the mastery of all these things. They couldn't have conquered me if my own heart hadn't first yielded. You mustn't stay here. (*Turning towards her with great tenderness.*) Oh, I'm glad that no stain rests upon you through me ——

AUDR. Don't trouble about me. I have been thinking of you. Your character?

MICH. My character! My character! My character!

AUDR. (*glances up at the place where the portrait had hung*). Where is she?

(*He points to the picture on the floor.*)

MICH. I daren't look at her. I must hide it until ——

AUDR. Until?

MICH. Until we have done what we can to atone for this.

AUDR. What?

MICH. Repent, confess, submit to any penance

that may be enjoined us. And then if and when it shall be permitted us — marriage.

AUDR. Marriage?

MICH. Retirement from all who know us, and lifelong consecration of ourselves to poverty and good works, so that at the last we may perhaps win forgiveness for what we have done.

AUDR. Marriage?

Re-enter ANDREW *with manuscripts.*

ANDR. I beg pardon. I thought Mrs. Lesden had gone. (*Puts manuscripts on table and is going off.*)

AUDR. I am just going, Mr. Gibbard.

ANDR. (*turns and speaks to her*). I met a stranger on the beach yesterday evening. He inquired for you and the way to your house.

AUDR. Indeed.

ANDR. He asked a great many questions about you.

AUDR. What questions?

ANDR. How you lived in this quiet place, and who were your friends, and where you were yesterday.

AUDR. Did he give his name?

ANDR. I didn't ask for it. I suppose he's staying in the place. I saw him at the door of the George later in the evening.

AUDR. One of my London friends, I suppose. What did you reply to his questions?

ANDR. I told him Mr. Feversham was one of your

friends, but as I didn't know where you were yesterday, of course I couldn't tell him, could I?
(*Looks at her, exit.*)

AUDR. Did you notice that?

MICH. Notice what?

AUDR. The look that man gave me as he went out. Does he suspect us?

MICH. Impossible.

AUDR. I feel sure he does. Send for him and question him at once. I'll go.

Enter FANNY *with a letter.*

FANNY. For you, ma'am.
(*Giving letter to* AUDRIE, *who glances at it, shows a sharp, frightened surprise, instantly concealed, and then stands motionless.*)

FANNY. The gentleman's waiting for an answer.

AUDR. (*very quiet, cold voice*). I'll come at once.
(*Exit* FANNY.)

MICH. What's the matter?

AUDR. Nothing. Question that man. Find out if he knows anything. I'll come back as soon as I can. (*Exit, without opening letter.*)

MICH. (*follows her to door, closes it after her, then goes to right door, calls*). Andrew.

Re-enter ANDREW.

MICH. What is this passage you're in difficulty about?

ANDR. (*comes to him with old manuscripts*). What's the matter?

MICH. My head is dizzy this morning.

ANDR. Didn't you say you couldn't sleep?

MICH. What time did you get back from Saint Margaret's yesterday?

ANDR. About twelve.

MICH. You saw my uncle off by the afternoon train?

ANDR. Yes.

MICH. And then? (ANDREW *does not reply*.) You were surprised to find me coming back with Withycombe instead of staying till Saturday?

ANDR. No.

MICH. Withycombe's message about the telegram a little disturbed me. (*A little pause, watching* ANDREW.) I thought perhaps Mrs. Lesden might have started to come to Saint Decuman's (*pause, still watching* ANDREW), and been lost on the way.

ANDR. Did you?

MICH. She is such a strange, flighty creature, that I should scarcely be surprised at anything she took it into her head to do.

ANDR. (*looking him full in the face*). She went up to London, didn't she?

MICH. (*wincing a little*). Yes.

ANDR. And came back through the night by the mail?

MICH. Yes. Why do you look at me like that?

ANDR. I beg your pardon. Is there any other question you'd like to ask me?

MICH. Question? About what?

ANDR. About Mrs. Lesden — or anything that's troubling you.

MICH. Troubling me? I'm not troubled about anything.

ANDR. Oh! I thought perhaps you were. (*Going.*)

MICH. Andrew. (ANDREW *stops.*) I've been thinking about — about Rose.

ANDR. Have you?

MICH. Perhaps I was wrong in urging her to confess.

ANDR. It isn't much good thinking that now, is it?

MICH. No, except to ask you to forgive me, and to say that you don't cherish any ill-feeling against me on that account.

ANDR. I forgive you, and I don't cherish any ill-feeling against you on that or any account.

MICH. I may trust you entirely, Andrew?

ANDR. If you doubt it — try me.

MICH. Try you?

ANDR. Didn't I tell you to ask me any question you like?

MICH. (*alarmed*). What do you mean? (*Pause, looks at* ANDREW.) Enough. I trust you absolutely — (*looks at him*) — in everything.

ANDR. You may. (*Is again going.*)

MICH. No, Andrew, nothing has occurred — I was

afraid — it seemed so strange — this telegram business. What are you thinking about me?

ANDR. Take care, sir. Don't betray yourself to anybody but me.

MICH. Betray myself?

ANDR. You're a worse bungler at lying than I was. Don't look like that, or other people will guess. Don't give way. You're safe. Nobody but me suspects anything. Your character is quite safe — her character is quite safe. They're both in my keeping.

MICH. (*stares helplessly at him*). How did you know?

ANDR. I've suspected for some time past ——

MICH. You were wrong. There was nothing to suspect. It was a chance, an accident — there was no intention to deceive. What made you guess?

ANDR. When Withycombe brought the telegram to me I guessed something was wrong. I heard you go out in the middle of the night. I followed you down to the beach; I saw you put off; I waited for you to come back. I was on the top of the cliff just above you when you landed with her. I saw you come on here, and I watched her take the road to the station, and saw her come back to her home as if she had come in by the early morning train.

MICH. What are you going to do?

ANDR. Nothing. Don't I owe everything I am and everything I have in this world to you? I shall never breathe a word of what I know to a living soul.

MICH. Thank you, Andrew. Thank you. And you'll be sure above all that she is safe ——

ANDR. As safe as if I were in the grave. You go your way, just the same as if I didn't know.

MICH. Andrew.

ANDR. (*comes back*). Sir ——

MICH. (*breaking down*). I was harsh and cruel to Rose. I punished her more than she deserved. I was a hard, self-righteous priest! I hadn't been tempted myself then. Send for her to come home again! Comfort her and give her the best place in your heart. Write at once. Let her come back to-morrow! Oh, what weak, wretched Pharisees we are! What masks of holiness we wear! What whited sepulchres we are! Send for her! Make up to her for all she has suffered! Let me ask her pardon! Oh, Andrew, have pity on me! Forgive me, forgive me!

(*Bending his head in tears.* ANDREW *steals out of the room. A long pause.* AUDRIE *appears at window in the same place as in Act I., looks in, sees him, taps the window, he goes up to it.*)

AUDR. Let me in. Quickly. I want to speak to you.

(*He goes to door, opens it; a moment later she enters.*)

MICH. Well?

AUDR. Why didn't you take my warning? Why didn't you beat me, drive me, hound me away from you as I told you?

MICH. What now?

AUDR. Say you'll forgive me before I tell you! No, don't forgive me!

MICH. I don't understand you. Is anything discovered?

AUDR. What does that matter? Oh, don't hate me. If you say one unkind word to me I shall kill myself. Read the letter which came here to me just now. (*He takes the letter wonderingly.*)

MICH. Whom did it come from?

AUDR. My husband.

MICH. Your husband? (*She nods.*) Your husband! He is alive? (*She nods.*)

AUDR. (*with a laugh*). Didn't I tell you I should ruin you body and soul? (*He stands overwhelmed.*) Why do you stand there? Why don't you do something? (*Laughing at him.*) I say, ghostly father, we make a pretty pair, you and I, don't we? What shall we do? Confess in white sheets and candles together, you and I? Why don't you do something — (*Laughing at him.*) And you stand there like a stone saint. (*Comes up to him.*) Kill me and have done with me!

MICH. You said your husband died after two years.

AUDR. I said I never saw him again — alive. I thought then that I never should.

MICH. But — you believed he was dead. You believed he was dead — (*She does not reply.*) You didn't know the night before last that your husband was living?

AUDR. Don't I tell you to kill me and have done with it.

MICH. (*horrified*). You knew he was living?

AUDR. (*very imploringly*). I love you, I love you. Say one word to me! Say one word to me! Say you forgive me.

MICH. I forgive you. (*Stands overwhelmed.*) Take this letter —— (*Offering it.*)

AUDR. I didn't mean to do this. Do make excuses for me. We lived unhappily together. When I came into all my money I bargained with him that we would never see each other again. It was a fair bargain — a contract. He went away to America — I gave out he was dead. From that time to this I have never had a thought of his return. He was dead to me. He has no right to come and spoil my life. Read that letter from him.

MICH. No — take it. (*Gives the letter back.*)

AUDR. Tell me what to do.

MICH. I'm not fit to advise you.

AUDR. What can we do?

MICH. I don't know. We're in a blind alley with our sin. There's no way out of this.

AUDR. I shall defy him.

MICH. No.

AUDR. Yes. A bargain's a bargain. I shall go back and defy him. I'll never see him again. But then — what then? What will you do?

MICH. Don't think of me.

AUDR. Speak to me. Say one word. Oh, it has been on the tip of my tongue so many times to tell you all, but I couldn't bear to lose your love, so I deceived you. (*He walks about perplexed. She goes to him very gently and coaxingly.*) Say you aren't sorry — say that deep down in your inmost heart you aren't sorry for what is past!

MICH. Sorry? No. God forgive me. I'm not sorry. I can't be sorry. I wish I could.

AUDR. (*coming to him*). Ah, now I know you love me! If you only dare be as bold as I dare ——

MICH. Bold?

AUDR. We love each other. Our loves and lives are in our own hands.

MICH. (*repulses her, braces himself to stern resolve, very coldly and commandingly*). Listen! These are perhaps the last words I shall ever speak to you. The past is past. There's no way out of that. But the future is in our power. Can't you see, woman, that we are half-way down the precipice? We'll go no further. From this moment we part; I toil back to repentance and peace one way, you toil back another. So far as God will give me grace I'll never think of you from this moment — I'll spend all my life in putting a gulf between you and me. You do the same — ask only one thing for yourself and me, that we may forget each other.

AUDR. (*looks at him, smiles, sighs, then as she is going off*). I was right about man's love. You are all cowards. There's not one of you that doesn't think first of his comfort, or his pocket, or his honour, or his skin, or his soul, and second of the woman he thinks he loves. Forget you? (*A little laugh.*) Do you think that possible? Do you think I was jesting with you when I gave myself to you? Forget you? (*A little laugh.*) My memory is good for such trifles. Forget you?

MICH. (*with a wild revulsion*). Oh, take me where you will! I have no guide but you! Heaven, hell, wherever you go, I shall follow. Be sure of that. But won't you be my better angel, now I've lost her: If you love me as you say, you can yet be the master influence of my life, you can yet save yourself through me, and me through you. Won't you make our love a monument for good? Dearest of all, I'm at your feet — I think you come from heaven, and I'm all obedience to you. You are my angel. Lead me — Lead me, not back to sin — Lead me towards heaven — You can even now!

AUDR. What do you wish me to do?

MICH. Go back to your duty and to deep repentance. Have strength, dearest. These are not idle words — duty, purity, holiness. They mean something. Love is nothing without them. Have courage to tread the hard road. Leave me.

AUDR. If I leave you now, shall we meet one day — hereafter?

MICH. Yes.

AUDR. You're sure? You do believe it?
MICH. With all my heart.
AUDR. And you'll stay here and carry on your work, restore the Minster, and let me think that I'm helping you.
MICH. I can't do that now.
AUDR. Yes.
MICH. No.
AUDR. Yes.
MICH. But with that money — your money!
AUDR. Many churches are built with sinners' money. Do this for me.
MICH. If I dared — if it would come to good. — You know how dear a hope it has been to me all my life through.
AUDR. Do it, because I ask it. You will?
MICH. And you'll leave me, leave this place, because I ask it. You will?
AUDR. I love you. I obey you.
      (*She comes to him.*)
MICH. No, I daren't come near to you. You'll go?
(*He opens the door; she passes out; re-enters.*)
AUDR. Listen to this. Whatever happens, I shall never belong to anybody but you. You understand? (MICHAEL *bows his head.*) I shall never belong to anybody but you, Mike.
> (*She goes out again. He closes door, goes up to window. She passes. He watches her off, stays there some moments.*)

Re-enter ANDREW. MICHAEL *comes from window; the two men stand looking at each other.*

ANDR. You won't begin work this morning, I suppose?

MICH. (*firmly*). Yes. (*Goes to table, motions* ANDREW *to one chair, seats himself opposite. They take up the manuscripts.*) Where is the place?

ANDR. Fifty-first psalm, verse three. (MICHAEL *winces, turns over the manuscript.*) Have you found it? What are you looking at?

MICH. (*gets up suddenly*). I can't bear it.

ANDR. Can't bear what?

(MICHAEL *stands looking at him with terror.*)

ANDR. (*rises, comes to him*). Don't I tell you that all is safe. I shan't blab. Nobody shall ever know.

MICH. But *you* know!

ANDR. I shall never remind you of it.

MICH. But you do, you do! Your presence reminds me.

ANDR. Shall I leave you now and come again by-and-by?

MICH. (*with an effort*). No, stay. (*Points to seat.* ANDREW *seats himself.*) You've sent for Rose to come home?

ANDR. No.

MICH. No?

ANDR. I don't want to have her in this place where everybody knows about her.

MICH. Won't you send for her, Andrew — to please me?

ANDR. She's well enough where she is. (*Pointing to the manuscripts.*) Shall we go on?

MICH. What ought I to do, Andrew?

ANDR. Don't you know what you ought to do?

MICH. What?

ANDR. Mete out to yourself the same measure you meted to others.

MICH. Confess — in public. I can't! I can't! I daren't! I'm a coward, a weak miserable coward! Don't judge me harshly, Andrew! Don't be hard on me! (*Covering his face with his hands.*)

ANDR. (*cold, firm*). Come, sir! shall we get on with our work? (*Reading manuscript.*) "For I acknowledge my transgressions, and my sin is ever before me."

(MICHAEL *uncovers his face and sits staring at* ANDREW, *who sits cold and grim on the other side of the table.*)

Very slow curtain.

(*A year passes between Acts III. and IV.*)

ACT IV

SCENE. — *The Chancel of the Minster church of Saint Decuman at Cleveheddon, a beautiful building of Decorated Gothic architecture with signs of recent restoration. The altar and reredos, approached by steps, face the audience, who take up the same position towards it as spectators in the nave would do. Behind the altar a long vista of columns, arches, roof, and stained glass windows. An organ is built in left wall of the chancel at a considerable height. On both sides of the chancel are handsome high carved oak stalls. A large open place in front of the altar steps is flanked on each side by the transepts, which run to right and left of spectators and are filled with chair seats so far as can be seen. A small door in the north wall of the left transept leads to the organ loft. The whole church is most lavishly decorated with banners, hangings, scrolls, and large frescoes, and is smothered with flowers as if in readiness for a church festival. Large brass candlesticks on altar with lighted candles. Time, about nine on an autumn night. An organ volun-*

tary is being played as curtain rises. Enter MICHAEL *from transept. He has aged much, is very pale and emaciated. The voluntary ceases and the organ boy, a lad about fifteen, comes from small door in wall of left transept.*

WALTER (*carelessly*). Good-night, sir.

MICH. (*stopping him, puts his hand on the boy's head*). Good-bye, Walter. (*Pause, still detaining him, with considerable feeling.*) Good-bye, my dear lad.

(*Sighs, moves away from him. The boy shows slight respectful surprise and exit along transept. The* Organist *with keys enters from the little door, looks round the church admiringly.*)

ORGANIST. Everything ready for the ceremony to-morrow?

MICH. Yes, I think, everything.

ORGANIST. I was just putting the finishing touches to my music. How beautiful the church looks! You must be very proud and happy now your work is complete.

MICH. Not quite complete. I've to put the finishing touches to my part — to-morrow.

ANDREW *enters rather suddenly from transept.*

ANDR. Can I speak to you for a moment?

ORGANIST. Good-night. (*Going.*)

MICH. (*detains him*). Thank you for all you have done for me, and for the church, and for her services.

(*Shakes hands warmly.* *Exit the* Organist *by transept.*)

MICH. Well?

ANDR. I thought you'd like to know — Mrs. Lesden has come back to Cleveheddon, and she has brought a lady friend with her.

MICH. I know.

ANDR. You've seen her?

(MICHAEL *looks at him with great dignity.*)

ANDR. I beg your pardon.

MICH. I've not seen her.

ANDR. I beg your pardon. It's no business of mine. (*Going.*)

MICH. (*quietly*). Yes, it is business of yours.

ANDR. What do you mean?

MICH. Haven't you made it the chief business of your life all this last year?

ANDR. How? I've kept my word. I've never reminded you of it.

MICH. You've never allowed me to forget it for a single moment. Every time you've spoken to me, or looked at me, or crossed the room, or passed the window, every time I've heard your step on the stairs, or your voice speaking to the servants, you've accused me. If you had been in my place I would have been very kind to you, Andrew.

ANDR. How did you treat my girl?

MICH. I did what I thought was best for her soul.

ANDR. Then why don't you do what is best for your own soul?

MICH. I shall.

(ANDREW *looks at* MICHAEL *in startled inquiry.*)

Enter by transept DOCWRAY *and* SIR LYOLF. SIR LYOLF *is in evening dress under summer overcoat.* DOCWRAY *points out the decorations to* SIR LYOLF.

ANDR. Why have you sent for Rose to come back to Cleveheddon?

MICH. I wish her to be present at the services to-morrow. She is almost due. Go to the station and meet her. Bring her to me here.

(SIR LYOLF *and* DOCWRAY *saunter up towards* MICHAEL *and* ANDREW. ANDREW *stands perplexed.*)

MICH. (*firmly, to* ANDREW). Bring her to me here.

(ANDREW *goes off through transept, turns to look at* MICHAEL *before he goes off.*)

SIR LYOLF. You didn't turn up at dinner?

MICH. I was too busy.

SIR LYOLF. All prepared for to-morrow?

MICH. Yes, I think.

SIR LYOLF. So it seems Mrs. Lesden has come down from town.

MICH. So I understand.

SIR LYOLF (MICHAEL *is listening intently*). I thought we had seen the last of her when the long-lost husband returned and took her off to London. By the way, what has become of her husband?

MARK. He has gone back to South America.

(MICHAEL *is listening intently*.)

SIR LYOLF. Gone back to South America?

MARK. He only stayed three weeks in England. It is said that she has pensioned him off — he is to keep to his hemisphere, and she is to keep to hers.

SIR LYOLF. I don't like it!

MARK. Don't like what?

SIR LYOLF. I don't like women who pension off their husbands to live in South America.

MICH. Do you see much of her in town?

MARK. Not much. About every two months she sweeps into church in a whirlwind of finery and perfume, gives me a ridiculously large sum for the offertory, makes some most irreverent joke, or else pretends to be deeply religious ——

MICH. Pretends?

MARK. What can it be but pretence? Look at her life this last year.

MICH. What of it?

MARK. It has been one continual round of gaiety and excitement except when she was ill.

MICH. She has been ill?

MARK. Yes, and no wonder.

MICH. Why?

MARK. She goes everywhere, gives the most extravagant parties, mixes with the fastest, emptiest, London set. And she has taken for her companion a silly, flighty little woman, Mrs. Cantelo.

Sir Lyolf. I don't like it! Why has she come back to Cleveheddon just now?

Mark. To be present at the dedication service to-morrow, I suppose.

Sir Lyolf. Michael ——

Mich. Well?

Sir Lyolf. You know that everybody is asking where all the money came from for these magnificent restorations?

Mich. It was sent to me anonymously. The giver wishes to remain unknown.

Sir Lyolf. Yes! Yes! That's what you've told us. But of course you know who it is?

Mich. I mustn't speak of it.

Sir Lyolf. Forgive me.

Mich. Let's say no more. I'm glad you came here to-night. I've been very much perplexed by a confession that has been made to me recently. A priest — you know him, Mark — he is to be present to-morrow — a priest some time ago discovered one of his people in a course of lying and deception, and insisted upon a very severe penalty from the man. And now the priest tells me, that in order to save one very dear to him, he himself has lately been practising exactly the same course of lying and deception. He came to me for advice. I said, " You must pay exactly the same penalty that you demanded from your parishioner." But he objects — he says it will bring disgrace on his family, and disgrace on our cloth. He urged all manner of excuses, but I wouldn't listen to him. He wishes to be present at the dedication service to-morrow. I've refused him. Have I done right?

SIR LYOLF. Yes, I should say so.

MARK. Was it a just penalty?

MICH. Yes, I believe so — the just, the only penalty, in my opinion. Have I done right?

MARK. Yes, certainly.

MICH. I'm glad you both think that. To-morrow before the dedication service begins, I shall stand where I'm standing now and confess that I have been guilty of deadly sin and deceit. Then I shall go out from this place and never return.

(*They come away from him, staring at him in speechless surprise for some moments.*)

SIR LYOLF. But — Good Heaven! — what have you done?

MICH. (*after a long pause*). Guess.

SIR LYOLF. But you won't proclaim yourself?

MICH. Yes.

SIR LYOLF. But your career — your reputation — your opportunities of doing good ——

MARK. Have you thought what this will mean to you, to us, to the church?

MICH. I have thought of nothing else for many months past.

Sir Lyolf. Surely there must be some way to avoid a public declaration. (Michael *shakes his head.*) You know I don't speak for myself. My day is nearly done, but you're in the full vigour of life, with a great reputation to sustain and increase. Don't do this — for my sake, for your own sake, for the sake of Heaven, don't do it!

Mich. I must.

Mark. What are the circumstances?

Mich. I can't tell you. I wouldn't have told you so much except that I knew I might trust both of you never to hint or whisper anything against — against any but myself. If you should guess — as most likely you will — the name of my companion in sin, it will never cross your lips? I may ask that of you?

Sir Lyolf. You know you may.

Mark. Of course we shall say nothing.

Sir Lyolf. But — but —— (*Sits down overwhelmed.*)

Mark. Can't we talk this over further? Have you considered everything?

Mich. Everything. I have known for many months that this must come. I have tried to palter and spare myself, but each time the conviction has returned with greater and greater force, "You must do it there, and then, and in that way."

Mark. But you've repented?

Mich. Most deeply. I have fasted and prayed. I have worn a hair shirt close to my skin. But my sin remains. It isn't rooted out of my heart. I can't get rid of its image.

MARK. Its image?

MICH. (*same calm, tranquil, matter-of-fact tone*). I believe that every sin has its exact physical image. That just as man is the expression of the thought of God, so our own thoughts and desires and aims, both good and bad, have somewhere or the other their exact material counterpart, their embodiment. The image of my sin is a reptile, a greyish-green reptile, with spikes, and cold eyes without lids. It's more horrible than any creature that was ever seen. It comes and sits in my heart and watches me with those cold eyes that never shut, and never sleep, and never pity. At first it came only very seldom; these last few months it has scarcely left me day or night, only at night it's deadlier and more distorted and weighs more upon me. It's not fancy. Mark, I know, I know, that if I do not get rid of my sin, my hell will be to have that thing sitting beside me for ever and ever, watching me with its cold eyes. But (*hopefully*) I shall be rid of it after to-morrow.

MARK. My poor fellow!

SIR LYOLF (*rising, coming back to* MICHAEL). Michael, can't you postpone this? Can't it be at some other time? Not in the very hour which should be the proudest and happiest of your life?

MICH. There is no other hour, no other way. (*Looks at them both, takes both their hands affection-*

ately.) Tell me (*very piteously*) that you neither of you love me the less,—or at least say that you love me a little still, after what I've told you.

SIR LYOLF. Don't you know?

MARK. How can you ask that?

  ANDREW *and* ROSE *appear in the transept.*

MICH. (*to* ANDREW). One moment, Andrew. (*To his father.*) I've a word or two to say to Andrew.

SIR LYOLF. Come and stay the night with me and let us talk this over.

MICH. No, I must be alone to-night. Good-night, dear Mark.   (MARK *wrings his hand.*)

SIR LYOLF. You are resolved to go through with this? It must be? (MICHAEL *bows his head.*)

SIR LYOLF. I can't be here to-morrow. I couldn't face it. But (*with great affection*) I shan't be far away when you want me. (*Very warm handshake.*) Come, Mr. Docwray.

  (*Exeunt* SIR LYOLF *and* DOCWRAY *by transept.*)

ANDR. (*bringing* ROSE *to* MICHAEL). I've brought her.

  (ROSE *is in an Anglican sister's dress; she is very pale and her manner is subdued. She comes slowly and reverently to* MICHAEL, *and is going to bend to him. He takes her hands and raises her.*)

MICH. No. You mustn't bend to me. I've sent for you, Rose, to ask your pardon.

Rose. My pardon?

Mich. I made you pass through a terrible ordeal last year. Will you forgive me?

Rose. What should I forgive? You were right. You said it would bring me great peace. And so it has — great peace.

Mich. And you wouldn't undo that morning's work?

Rose. No. It seems I died that morning and left all my old life in a grave. This is quite a new life. I wouldn't change it.

Mich. Andrew, do you hear that?

Andr. Yes.

Mich. I was right, then? I was right? You are happy?

Rose. Yes, I am happy — at least, I'm peaceful, and peace is better than happiness, isn't it?

Mich. Yes, peace is best! Peace is best! I shall find it too, some day. Andrew, she has forgiven me. Can't you forgive me? We may never see each other again on this side the grave. Don't let us part in anger!

Andr. Part?

Mich. As soon as I can arrange my affairs I shall leave Cleveheddon.

Andr. But your work?

Mich. My work is ended. I'll see that you and Rose are sufficiently provided for.

(*Taking their hands, trying to join them;* Andrew *holds aloof.*)

Andr. No. I can't take any favour from you.

Mich. It's no favour. I've trained you to a special work which has unfitted you for everything else. It is my duty to provide for your old age.

Andr. I can't take any favour from you.

Mich. Old comrade (*leaning on* Andrew's *shoulder;* Andrew *draws away*), old comrade (*draws* Andrew *to him*), we had many happy days together in the summer of our life. Now the autumn has come, now the winter is coming, I'm setting out on a cold, dark journey. Won't you light a little flame in our old lamp of friendship to cheer me on my way? You'll take my gift — you'll take it, and make a home for her?

Andr. (*bursts out*). You'll break my heart with your kindness! I don't deserve it! I was a half-bred, starving dog. You took me in, and, like the hound I am, I turned and bit the hand that fed me. Let me be! Let me be!

Mich. Rose, speak to him.

Rose. Father, you are grieving Mr. Feversham.

Andr. I'll do whatever you tell me. But don't forgive me.

Mich. Take him home, Rose. I parted you. Let me think I have restored you to each other.

(*Joining them.*)

Andr. (*to* Michael). I can't say anything to-night. I never was good enough to black your shoes. I can't thank you. I can't speak. Good-night. Come, Rose!

ACT IV   MICHAEL AND HIS LOST ANGEL   85

(MICHAEL *shakes* ROSE'S *hand very tenderly. Exeunt* ROSE *and* ANDREW *by transept.* MICHAEL *watches them off, goes to altar.*)

MICH. (*alone*). One thing more and all is done. (*Looking round the church.*) And I must give you up ! Never enter your doors, never lead my people through you in chariots of fire, never make you the very presence-chamber of God to my soul and their souls who were committed to me! Oh, if I had been worthy!

(*A little pause. A woman's laugh is heard in the transept opposite to that by which* ANDREW *and* ROSE *have gone off.* MICHAEL *withdraws to the side of chancel, where he is seen by the audience, during the following scene, but is hidden from* AUDRIE *and* MRS. CANTELO.)

AUDRIE *enters from transept in magnificent evening dress, cloak, and jewellery, and carrying a large basket of roses. Her features are much paler and sharpened, and she shows a constant restlessness and excitement.*

AUDR. (*looks round, calls out*). Somebody is here? (*Pause, calls out.*) Somebody is here? No? (*Speaks down transept.*) You may come in, Milly.

MILLY CANTELO, *a fashionable little woman, enters at transept, looking admiringly round the church.*

AUDR. There's nobody here except (*raising her voice*) a stone saint (*pointing up to carved figure*), and he can't hear, because he has only stone ears, and he can't feel, because he has only a stone heart.

(MICHAEL *shows intense feeling.*)

MILLY (*looking round*). Isn't it gorgeous?

AUDR. H'm — yes ——(*Raises her voice.*) I can't bear that stone saint. Look how hard and lifeless he is. In a well-regulated world there would be no room for angels or devils, or stone saints, or any such griffins.

MILLY. Audrie, you are queer to-night. You'll be ill again.

AUDR. I hope so.

MILLY. What's the matter with you?

AUDR. Life's the matter with me, I think. I've got it badly, and I don't know how to cure myself.

MILLY. I wish you wouldn't talk nonsense, and run about on silly errands in the dark.

AUDR. I won't for long. When my head is tightly bandaged in a white cloth, I can't talk any more nonsense, can I? And when my feet are comfortably tucked up in my final night-gown I can't run after stone saints in the dark, can I?

MILLY. Oh, you give me the creeps. I can't imagine why you wanted to come out to-night.

AUDR. To decorate the church.

MILLY. Don't you think it's decorated enough?

AUDR. (*looking*). No, it wants a few more touches. I must just titivate a cherub's nose, or hang a garland on an apostle's toe, just to show my deep, deep devotion ——

MILLY. Your deep, deep devotion?

AUDR. My deep, deep love, my deep, deep worship, my deep, deep remembrance.

MILLY. Of what?

AUDR. The church, of course.

MILLY. What a heap of money all this must have cost! Who gave it all?

AUDR. I gave two hundred pounds when I lived here last year.

MILLY. I wonder who gave all the rest!

AUDR. I wonder!

MILLY. Mr. Feversham must have some very devoted friends.

AUDR. So it seems.

MILLY. Did you know him very well when you lived here?

AUDR. Not very well.

MILLY. What sort of a man is he?

AUDR. Oh, a very cold, distant man — a good deal of the priest about him, and as much feeling as that stone figure up there.

MILLY. You didn't like him?

AUDR. Oh, I liked him well enough. But I don't think he cared much for me. I dare say he has forgotten all about me by this time. Milly ——
         (*Bursts into tears.*)

MILLY. What is it?

AUDR. I'm not well to-night. I oughtn't to have come here. Milly — I never forget anybody. If I had once loved you I should love you for ever. If you were wicked, or unfortunate, or unfaithful, it would make no difference to me. Kiss me, Milly — say you believe me.

Milly. You know I do, darling.

Audr. (*very passionately*). I can be constant, Milly — I can! Constant in my friendship, constant in my love! Oh, Milly, I'm the most wretched woman in the world!

Milly. You're hysterical, dear.

Audr. No, I'm forsaken. Nobody loves me!
    (*Sobbing. Gesture from* Michael.)

Milly. Poor Audrie!

Audr. Let me be a few minutes by myself. I want to be quite alone. Go home and wait for me there.

Milly. I don't like leaving you.

Audr. (*getting her off at transept*). Yes — go, dear. I shall be better soon. Do leave me.

Milly. You won't be long?

Audr. No — I'll come soon.

 (*Accompanying her along transept. Exit* Milly *by transept.* Audrie *stands listening.* Michael *comes forward a step or two.*)

Audr. (*in the transept*). Are you there?

 (*He comes forward; she goes towards him; they stand for a moment or two looking at each other.*)

Audr. Are you deaf? I thought it was only your memory that was gone.

Mich. Why have you come here?

Audr. Mayn't I come into my own church? And such a sinner as I am?

Mich. Forgive me. You know how welcome I would make you — if I dared.

Audr. Then you don't dare? Then I'm not welcome?

Mich. (*troubled*). Yes! Yes! Very welcome! The Church owes much to you.

Audr. I think she does, for she has robbed me of your love. Why have you sent back all my letters unopened?

Mich. Can't you guess what it cost me to return them? (*Pause.*) What have you been doing all this last year?

Audr. Doing? Eating my heart. Racing through my life to get to the end of it. Skipping and chattering from Hyde Park Corner to the Inferno by a new short cut. What have you been doing?

Mich. Trying to repent and to forget.

Audr. Ah, well — I haven't been wasting my time quite so foolishly as you after all.

Mich. Will you never be serious?

Audr. Yes — soon.

Mich. You've been ill?

Audr. Oh, my dear spiritual doctor, you don't know how ill I've been. I get up every morning without hope, I drag through the day without hope, I go to this thing and that, to this party, to that reception, to the theatre, to church, to a pigeon-shooting match, to the park, to Ascot, to Henley — here, there, everywhere, all without hope.

MICH. What is it you want?

AUDR. I want to live again! I've never lived but those few months when we were learning to love each other! I want to feel that fierce breeze on my cheek that blew us together! Do you remember when we stood on the cliff hand in hand? And we shrieked and laughed down the wind like mad children? Do you remember?

MICH. No.

AUDR. No? Nor the wonderful pale sunrise, with the lemon and green lakes of light, and then the path of diamonds all across the sea? Don't you remember?

MICH. No.

AUDR. How strange you don't remember! Oh, my God, if I could forget!

MICH. (*apart from her*). Oh, my God, if I could forget! (*A long pause. He comes to her.*) I have one awful thought — I am bound to you — There is but one of us — I never felt it more than at this moment — And yet the awful thought comes to me — if by any decree we should be put asunder hereafter — if we should be parted then!

AUDR. Don't you dread being parted now — now this moment? Don't you dread being unhappy here — here on this earth?

MICH. I will not think of that. I have vowed!

AUDR. You don't love me! You don't love me! You don't love me!

MICH. If I had ten thousand worlds I'd sell them all and buy your soul. But I will keep the vow I have vowed. You are the holiest thing on earth to me. I will keep you white and stainless from me.

AUDR. You'll never forget me.

MICH. I have forgotten you.

AUDR. You'll never forget me.

MICH. (*same cold tone, going up the altar steps*). I have forgotten you.

(*Stands with his back to her for a few moments.*)

AUDR. (*with a gesture of resignation*). You'll let me put a bunch or two of flowers about the church before I go?

MICH. If I asked you not——

AUDR. I should obey you.

MICH. I do ask you not——

AUDR. Very well. It's hard lines that I mayn't decorate my own church.

MICH. I have another request to make — a favour to beg of you.

AUDR. It's done, whatever it is. But make it some great thing — something very hard and desperate, that I may show you there's nothing I would not do if you ask it.

MICH. It's something very simple. I'm going to ask you not to be present at the dedication service to-morrow.

AUDR. But I came on purpose ——

MICH. I beg you not. I have a strong reason. You won't come?

AUDR. Not if you wish me to stay away. Shall I see you after to-morrow?

MICH. After to-morrow I leave Cleveheddon for ever.

AUDR. Where are you going?

MICH. I don't know.

AUDR. It doesn't matter, I shall find you out.

MICH. You'll follow me?

AUDR. Yes — all over this world, and the ten thousand others. I shall follow you. You'll find me always with you, clawing at your heart. Au revoir. (*Takes up her basket of roses, going out with them by transept, stops.*) Do let me put some flowers on the altar — just to remind you. Your memory is so bad, you know.

>(*He raises his hand very quietly and turns his back on her. She stands very quiet and hopeless for a few seconds, then takes up the basket of flowers, goes a step or two towards transept, turns.*)

AUDR. I'm going to be very ill after this. (*He stands at altar in an attitude of prayer, his back to her.*) Do you hear, I'm going to be very ill? There's a little string in my heart — I've just heard it snap. (*Pause.*) If I were dying and I sent for you, would you come?

MICH. (*after a long pause, very quietly*). Yes.
(*Pause.*)
AUDR. And that's all? And that's all? (*He stands unmoved at altar, his back to her. She takes a large red rose out of the basket, throws it towards him; it falls on the white marble altar steps.*) There's a flower for to-morrow! Do put it on the altar for me! You won't? You won't? (*No answer.*) It is hard to be turned out of my own church— It is hard——

>(*Exit* AUDRIE *by transept with the basket of flowers. A sob is heard,* MICHAEL *turns round. A door is heard to close. He puts out the altar lights, throws himself on altar steps. The curtains fall.*
>
>*The falling of the curtains signifies the passing of the night.*
>
>*A peal of joyous church bells followed by organ music and singing. The curtain rises and discovers the church in broad daylight and filled with worshippers.* ANDREW *and* ROSE *are at the corner in prominent positions.* AU-DRIE'S *flower is lying on the altar steps. A processional hymn is being sung. A procession of surpliced priests file up the aisle and take their places in the chancel, walking over* AUDRIE'S *rose.* MICHAEL *follows at the end of the procession; as he reaches the altar steps, he turns, very pale and cold, and speaks in a low, calm voice.*)

MICH. Before this service begins and this church is re-consecrated I have a duty to perform to my people. (*Great attention of all.*) I have often insisted in this place on the necessity of a life of perfect openness before God and man. I have taught you that your lives should be crystal clear, that your hearts should be filled with sunlight, so that no foul thing may hide therein. I have enforced that with others, because I believe with my heart and soul that it is the foundation of all wholesome and happy human life. I stand here to affirm it to-day in the presence of God and you all. I stand here to affirm it against myself as I formerly affirmed it against another. I stand here to own to you that while I have been vainly preaching to you, my own life has been polluted with deceit and with deadly sin. I can find no repentance and no peace till I have freely acknowledged to you all that I am not worthy to continue my sacred office, not worthy to be the channel of grace to you. It was the dearest wish of my life to restore this beautiful temple, and to be Heaven's vicar here. I have raised it again, but I may not enter. I dare not enter. I have sinned — as David sinned. I have broken the sanctity of the marriage vow. It is my just sentence to go forth from you, not as your guide, your leader, your priest; but as a broken sinner, humbled in the dust before the Heaven he has offended. I bid you all farewell. I ask your pardon for having dared to continue in my office knowing I had profaned and desecrated it. It now remains for me to seek the pardon of Heaven. Let the service continue without me. Let no one leave his place. Pray for me all of you! I have need of your prayers! Pray for me!

> (*He comes down from the altar steps amidst the hushed and respectful surprise of the congregation, who all turn to look at him as he passes.* ROSE *makes a very slight gesture of sympathy as he passes her.* ANDREW *stands with hands over his eyes.* MICHAEL *passes out by transept, his head bowed, his lips moving in prayer as he goes off.*)

Curtain.

(*Ten months pass between Acts IV. and V.*)

ACT V

SCENE.—*Reception room of the Monastery of San Salvatore at Majano, in Italy. A simply furnished room in an old Italian building. At back right an open door approached by a flight of steps, at back left a large window; a mass of masonry divides the window and door. A door down stage, left. The portrait of* MICHAEL'S *mother hangs on the wall. Time, a summer evening. Discover* FATHER HILARY *reading. Enter* SIR LYOLF *up the steps and by door at back.*

FATHER H. Well?

SIR LYOLF. I've been to see her again. I can't get her out of my mind.

FATHER H. How is she this evening?

SIR LYOLF. In the very strangest state, laughing, crying, jesting, fainting, and chattering like a magpie. I believe she's dying.

FATHER H. Dying?

SIR LYOLF. Yes. It seems she had a kind of malarial fever a month or two ago and wasn't properly treated. I wish there was a good English doctor in the place. And I wish Michael was here.

FATHER H. Be thankful that he is away.

SIR LYOLF. But if he finds out that she has been here, that she has sent again and again for him, and that we have hidden it from him — and that she has died?

FATHER H. He mustn't know it until he can bear to hear it. We must consider him first. Think what he must have suffered all these months. Now that at last he is learning to forget her, now that he is finding peace, how wrong, how cruel it would be to re-open his wounds!

SIR LYOLF. She said he promised to come to her if she sent for him. She begged so hard. She has come from England with the one hope of seeing him. I felt all the while that I was helping to crush the life out of her.

FATHER H. What did you tell her?

SIR LYOLF. That he had gone away alone for a few days in the mountains. That we didn't exactly know where to find him, but that he might come back at any time, and that I would bring him to her the moment he returned.

FATHER H. Well, what more can we do?

SIR LYOLF. Nothing now, I suppose. I wish we had sent after him when she came last week. We could have found him before this. Besides, she doesn't believe me.

FATHER H. Doesn't believe you?

SIR LYOLF. She thinks that Michael is here with

us, and that we are hiding it from him. I wish he'd come back.

FATHER H. If she is passing away, better it should all be over before he returns.

SIR LYOLF. I don't like parting them at the last. She loves him, Ned, she loves him.

FATHER H. Remember it's a guilty love.

SIR LYOLF. Yes, I know.

FATHER H. Remember what it has already cost him.

SIR LYOLF. Yes, I know. But love is love, and whether it comes from heaven, or whether it comes from the other place, there's no escaping it. I believe it always comes from heaven!

(FATHER HILARY *shakes his head.*)

SIR LYOLF. I'm getting my morals mixed up in my old age, I suppose. But, by God, she loves him, Ned, she loves him — Who's that?

(FATHER HILARY *looks out of window, makes a motion of silence.*)

FATHER H. Hush! He's come back.

SIR LYOLF. I must tell him.

FATHER H. Let us sound him first, and see what his feelings are. Then we can judge whether it will be wise to let him know.

Enter up steps and by door MICHAEL *in a travelling cloak. He enters very listlessly. He has an expression of settled pensiveness and resigna-*

tion, almost despair. He comes up very affectionately to his father, shakes hands, does the same to FATHER HILARY. *Then he sits down without speaking.*

SIR LYOLF. Have you come far to-day, Michael?

MICH. No, only from Casalta. I stayed there last night.

SIR LYOLF. You are back rather sooner than you expected?

MICH. I had nothing to keep me away. One place is the same as another.

FATHER H. And about the future? Have you made up your mind?

MICH. Yes. I had really decided before I went away, but I wanted this week alone to be quite sure of myself, to be quite sure that I was right in taking this final step, and that I should never draw back. (*To* FATHER HILARY.) You remember at Saint Decuman's Isle, two years ago, you said you could give me a deeper peace than I could find within or around me?

FATHER H. And I can. And I will.

MICH. Give me that peace. I need it. When can I be received?

FATHER H. When I have prepared you.

MICH. Let it be soon. Let it be soon. (*To his father.*) This is a blow to you——

SIR LYOLF. You know best. I wish you could have seen your way to stay in your own church.

MICH. I was an unfaithful steward and a disobedient son to her. She is well rid of me. (*To* FATHER HILARY.) You are sure you can give me that peace ——

FATHER H. If you'll but give me your will entirely, and let me break it in pieces. On no other condition. Come and talk to me alone.

(*Trying to lead him off left.*)

SIR LYOLF. No ——! (*Goes to* MICHAEL.) Michael, you are at peace now, aren't you?

(MICHAEL *looks at him.*)

FATHER H. He will be soon. Leave him to me.

SIR LYOLF. No. I must know the truth from him.

FATHER H. You're wrong to torture him.

SIR LYOLF (*to* MICHAEL). You are at peace now — at least, you are gaining peace, you are forgetting the past?

FATHER H. He will. He shall. Say no more. (*To* MICHAEL.) Come with me, — I insist!

SIR LYOLF. No. Michael, before you take this last step answer me one question — I have a reason for asking. Tell me this truly. If by any chance someone in England — someone who was dear to you ——

MICH. Oh, don't speak of her — (*Turns away, hides his head for a minute, turns round with a sudden outburst.*) Yes, speak of her! Speak of her! I haven't heard her name for so long! Let me hear it again — Audrie! Audrie!

FATHER H. (*sternly to* SIR LYOLF). Do you hear? Let him alone. Don't torment him by dragging up the past. He has buried it.

MICH. No! No! No! Why should I deceive you? Why should I deceive myself? All this pretended peace is no peace! There is no peace for me without her, either in this world or the next!

FATHER H. Hush! Hush! How dare you speak so!

MICH. I must. The live agony of speech is better than the dead agony of silence, the eternal days and nights without her! Forget her? I can't forget! Look!   (*Takes out a faded red rose.*)

SIR LYOLF. What is it?

MICH. A flower she threw me in church the last time I saw her. And I wouldn't take it! I sent her away! I sent her away! And her flower was trampled on. The next night I got up in the middle of the night and went over to the church and found it on the altar steps. I've kept it ever since. (*To his father.*) Talk to me about her. I want somebody to talk to me about her. Tell me something you remember of her — some little speech of hers. — Do talk to me about her.

SIR LYOLF. My poor fellow!

MICH. I can't forget. The past is always with me! I live in it. It's my life. You think I'm here in this place with you — I've never been here. I'm living with her two years ago. I have no present, no future. I've only the past when she was with me. Give me the past! Oh! give me back only one moment of that past, one look, one word from her — and then take all that remains of me and do what you like with it. Oh! (*Goes back to bench, sits.*)

SIR LYOLF (*to* FATHER HILARY). You see! I must tell him ——

FATHER H. No, not while he's in this mad state. Let's quiet him first.

SIR LYOLF. Then we'll take him to her!

FATHER H. When he is calmer.

SIR LYOLF. Take care it isn't too late.

FATHER H. (*goes to* MICHAEL, *puts his hand on* MICHAEL'S *shoulder*). This is weakness. Be more brave! Control yourself!

MICH. Have I not controlled myself? Who trained and guided himself with more care than I? Who worked as I worked, prayed as I prayed, kept watch over himself, denied himself, sacrificed himself as I did? And to what end? Who had higher aims and resolves than I? They were as high as heaven, and they've tumbled all round me! Look at my life, the inconsequence, the inconsistency, the futility, the foolishness of it all. What a patchwork of glory and shame! Control myself? Why? Let me alone! Let me drift! What does it matter where I go? I'm lost in the dark! One way is as good as another!

(*The vesper bell heard off at some little distance.*)

FATHER H. You've wandered away from the road, and now you complain that the maps are wrong.

Get back to the highway, and you'll find that the maps are right.

MICH. Forgive me, Uncle Ned — I'm ashamed of this. I shall get over it. I'll talk with you by and by. I will submit myself. I will be ruled. Father, come to me. You nursed me yourself night after night when I was delirious with the fever. I was a child then. I'm a child now. Talk to me about her. Talk to me about Audrie!

> (AUDRIE'S *face, wasted and hectic, appears just over the doorstep, coming up the steps at back; during the following conversation she raises herself very slowly and with great difficulty up the steps, leaning on the wall.*)

MICH. I've heard nothing of her. Where do you think she is? In England? I think I could be patient, I think I could bear my life if I knew for certain that all was well with her. If I could know that she is happy — No, she isn't happy — I know that.

SIR LYOLF. Michael, I've had some news of her.

MICH. News! Good? Bad? Quick! Tell me.

SIR LYOLF. You can bear it?

MICH. She's dead? And I never went to her! I never went to her! She won't forgive me!

SIR LYOLF. She's not dead.

MICH. What then?

SIR LYOLF. You promised you'd go to her if she sent for you.

MICH. Yes.

SIR LYOLF. She has sent for you. (*Sees her entering.*)

MICH. She's dying?

(*She has gained the door, just enters, leaning back against the post.* MICHAEL'S *back is towards her.*)

AUDR. I'm afraid I am.

(MICHAEL *looks at her, utters a wild cry of joy, then looks at her more closely, realizes she is dying, goes to her, kisses her, bursts into sobs.*)

AUDR. (*putting her hand on his head*). Don't cry. I'm past crying for. Help me there. (*Points to seat.*)

(*He seats her; looks at her with great anxiety.*)

AUDR. (*laughing, a little weak feeble laugh, and speaking feebly with pause between each word*). Don't pull — that — long — face. You'll — make me — laugh — if you — do. And I want to be — serious now.

MICH. But you're dying!

AUDR. (*with a sigh*). Yes. Can't help it. Sir Lyolf, pay — coachman — (*taking out purse feebly*) outside — No, perhaps — better — wait — or bring another sort — of — carriage. But no mutes — no feathers — no mummery.

SIR LYOLF. I'll send him away. You'll stay with us now?

AUDR. (*nods*). So sorry — to intrude. Won't be very long about it.

(*Exit* SIR LYOLF *by door and steps;* MICHAEL *is standing with hands over eyes.*)

FATHER H. (*coming to* AUDRIE). Can I be of any service, any comfort to you?

AUDR. No, thanks. I've been dreadfully wicked — doesn't much — matter, eh? Can't help it now. Haven't strength to feel sorry. So sorry I can't feel sorry.

FATHER H. There is forgiveness ——

AUDR. Yes, I know. Not now. Want to be with him.   (*Indicating* MICHAEL.)

SIR LYOLF *re-enters by steps.*

SIR LYOLF. Come, Ned ——

AUDR. (*to* FATHER HILARY). Come back again — in — few minutes. I shall want you. I've been dreadfully wicked. But I've built a church — and — (*feverishly*) I've loved him — with all my heart — and a little bit over.

(*Exeunt* SIR LYOLF *and* FATHER HILARY, *door left.*)

AUDR. (*motioning* MICHAEL). Why didn't you come when I sent for you?

MICH. I've only known this moment. Why didn't you send before?

AUDR. I sent you hundreds — of messages — from my heart of hearts. Didn't you get them?

MICH. Yes — every one.

AUDR. I've crawled all over Europe after you. And you aren't worth it — Yes, you are. You wouldn't come ——

MICH. Yes — anywhere — anywhere — take me where you will.

AUDR. You know — he's dead. I'm free.

MICH. Is it so? But it's too late.

AUDR. Yes. Pity! Not quite a well-arranged world, is it? Hold my hand. We're not to be parted?

MICH. No.

AUDR. Sure?

MICH. Quite sure. You're suffering?

AUDR. No — that's past — (*Shuts her eyes. He watches her.*) Very comfortable — very happy — just like going into a delicious faint — (*Sighs.*) Do you remember — beautiful sunrise — diamonds on the sea ——

MICH. Yes, I remember — all — every moment! And the wind that blew us together when we stood on the cliff! Oh! we were happy then — I remember all! All! All!

AUDR. So glad your memory's good at last. (*A vesper hymn heard off at some distance.*) Pity to die on such a lovely evening — not quite well-arranged world? But we were happy — if the next world has anything as good it won't be much amiss. I'm going. Fetch — priest — (MICHAEL *is going to door left; she calls him back.*) No. No time to waste. Don't leave me. We shan't be parted?

MICH. No! No! No! No!

AUDR. (*gives a deep sigh of content, then looks up at his mother's picture*). She's there? (MICHAEL *nods.*)

She'll forgive me! (*Blows a little kiss to the picture.*) But I'm your angel — I'm leading you ——

MICH. Yes. Where?

AUDR. I don't know. Don't fuss about it. "Le bon Dieu nous pardonnera : c'est son métier" — (*Closes her eyes.*) Not parted? (*Looks up at him.*)

MICH. No! No! No! No!

AUDR. You won't keep me waiting too long? (*Looks up at him, a long deep sigh of content.*) Hold my hand — Tight! tight! Oh! don't look so solemn ——

> (*Begins to laugh, a ripple of bright, feeble laughter, growing louder and stronger, a little outburst, then a sudden stop, as she drops dead.* MICHAEL *kisses her lips, her face, her hands, her dress.*)

Enter FATHER HILARY.

MICH. Take me! I give my life, my will, my soul, to you! Do what you please with me! I'll believe all, do all, suffer all — only — only persuade me that I shall meet her again!

(*Throws himself on her body.*)

CURTAIN.

Printed in the United Kingdom
by Lightning Source UK Ltd.
123697UK00001B/308/A